Operating Systems

Operating Systems

By

Archana Verma

KALPAZ

ISBN: 978-93-5324-949-6 (PB)

First Published, 2022

Published by

Kalpaz Publications
C-30, Satyawati Nagar,
Delhi – 110052
Ph.: 011-47034999, 9811692060
www.kalpazpublications.com
E-mail: kalpaz@hotmail.com

Printed at: Gyan Press, Delhi.

Dedicated

To

My Father

Sh. Vidya Sagar Verma

My Mother

Late Smt. Sudha Verma

My Sister

Dr. Vandana Verma Marwah

My Brother

Mr. Shashank Verma

My Brother-in-Law

Dr. Ashutosh Marwah

My Sister-in-Law

Mrs. Archana Devar Verma

My Daughter

Ritambhara

My Niece

Aparajita

My Nephew

Shreyas

My Nephew

Kartikeya

Contents

Preface

I was inspired to write this book out of passion and enthusiasm as I find this subject very interesting.

The book is primarily meant for MCA 1st year students of Dr. A.P.J. Abdul Kalam Technical University. The concepts have been explained in the way I perceive them. The diagrams, examples and thorough explanations are given to enhance the understanding of students.

The book contains introduction to operating systems, how processes work together, the role of central processing unit and memory management in running of programs, coupled with the input output unit.

It is hoped that the students will benefit from this book by having clear understanding of concepts.

Acknowledgements

My heartfelt thanks to Dr. O.P. Agarwal, Managing Director, NIET, Dr. Neema Agarwal, Additional Managing Director, NIET and Mr. Raman Batra, EVP, NIET for their blessings.

I would take this opportunity to thank Dr. Vinod M. Kapse, Director, NIET for his encouragement and guidance.

My sincere thanks to Dr. Ritesh Rastogi, Head of Department, Computer Applications, NIET for his good wishes and support.

I deeply thank Mr. B.P. Garg, Managing Director, Gyan Books, Mr. Amit Garg, Director, Gyan Books and their staff for publishing this book.

Last but not the least I would like to thank my students for their appreciation of my notes and lectures which encouraged me to write this book.

Chapter - 1

Introduction to Operating Systems

1.1 Introduction

An Operating System is an interface between the user and the hardware.

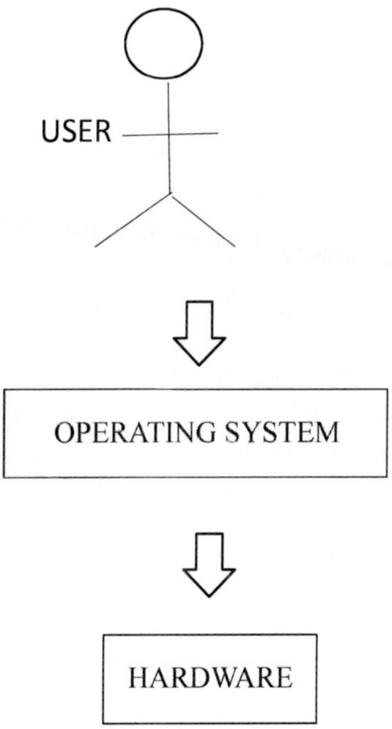

The operating system is a set of programs or software which is responsible to deal with the hardware. Suppose you are a user and you are sitting in front of your computer. Your computer consists of the hardware i.e. the keyboard, mouse, monitor and the CPU, or let us say you are sitting in front of your laptop. So you are the user and the laptop is the hardware.

Now how will the user start working with the Laptop, The screen which shows you icons is the software that is lying between you and the computer and that software is the operating system?

The most common types of operating systems are WINDOWS, Macintosh (Apple Computers), LINUX, UNIX and MS-DOS.

When you switch on your laptop with the power button, so what is happening inside the computer. The computer is booting up or starting itself, and when it is ready for you to work with, it shows you the desktop and the folders and the icons on the screen. And then you can use any one of them and start performing your work.

Have you ever wondered how does a computer start itself? You must have read in your earlier courses that there is a primary memory which is called the ROM i.e. Read-Only Memory. This ROM is manufactured at the factory and as its name suggests it can only be read. Nothing can be written on it. So the manufacturer prepares the instructions which are hard-wired onto this chip of ROM. And those instructions contain the way how the computer is going to be ready to work with. So when you press the power button on, the CPU reads instructions from the ROM and performs them one by one, and when they are complete then the system is ready for you to work with or in other words, the essential part of the operating system is loaded in the Ram (Random Access Memory) to start working with it. Since whenever you are going to start your computer, it will always be the same method so the instructions remain the same and they are put in the ROM. So every time a computer starts, it reads the same instructions from the ROM. Another Reason why ROM is hardwired and is not writable memory is that you do not want anybody to change the way you are going to start up your computer because if he changes, he may tamper the instructions and the computer might not be able to start itself. So, therefore, the instructions are hard-wired so that nobody can change them.

A formal definition of an operating system is a software or set of programs or routines which are mainly responsible for controlling the overall resources of the computer system.

An operating system is system software. There are two types of software, one is the application software and the other is the system software.

The system software is the set of programs which are mandatory for the system to function and which make the environment easy for the user to do work in. So that whatever application programs he writes, they may run smoothly. The system software comes with the hardware that you have purchased, be it the operating system or any other product such as ORACLE. But remember application software can also be purchased such as Microsoft office. This is application software and not system software. The main difference is that without the system software, your programs will not run, that is why it is the essential software, whereas without application software you will be able to run your programs.

Now examples of application software can vary from small simple C programs like writing a program of prime numbers or calculating the factorial of a number to large commercial applications such as airline reservation system, a banking application or computer games.

The examples of system software are types of operating systems such as Windows, Unix Dos. Apart from the operating systems they contain the compilers, interpreters or system libraries which contain commands which help to make the work easy for you, such as copy command, to copy one file to another, remove a file command or make a directory command etc.

1.2 Functions of an Operating System

As we have already said that the job of an operating system is to control the overall resources of the computer system, therefore, the resources of the computer system mean its memory unit, its Input-output unit and the central processing unit (CPU). So the operating system is responsible for:

(1) Memory Management
(2) Process Management
(3) File Management
(4) Input-Output Management
(5) Protection and Security
(6) Command Interpretation

Operating System is the overall manager and controller of the resources of the operating system and is responsible for making sure which Unit does what and in which order when to give control to which unit so that there are no clashes in the system's working.

1.2.1 Memory Management

When we write a program, it is written in the editor after that if we compile it and run it, it is loaded into the Primary Memory i.e. RAM, so that the memory manager part of the operating system is responsible for loading it into the RAM and then the CPU would need to execute each instruction of the machine code from the RAM. So the memory manager is responsible for transferring the data from the RAM to the CPU. Also if we save a file, which is written in the editor and we are saving it on the hard drive say C or D drive or on a pen drive (these are secondary memory storage devices), then also the memory manager part of the operating system is responsible for saving in the said drive. Also if we have already saved a file and we are now trying to run it, so we need to bring it from the secondary memory storage devices back into the RAM (Primary Memory). We need to bring it into the primary memory because the CPU only interacts with the primary memory that is the RAM.

Caching

A cache is a faster memory that resides between the CPU and the RAM. The CPU when has to execute any instruction taken from the RAM will check the cache first. If the instruction is present in the cache, it will take it from there, otherwise, if it is not present then it will contact the RAM.

Initially, the cache is empty, when CPU fetches an instruction from RAM, it sees that the cache is empty so goes to the RAM, puts the instruction in the cache and works on the instruction. Then when it needs the next instruction, it again first checks the cache, if the instruction is not there it goes to the RAM and puts it in the cache as well as works on it. In this way, the cache gets filled with some instructions. Suppose it needs an instruction now which is present in the cache, then the CPU will not go to the RAM but fetch it from the cache and work on it.

In this way, the cache is utilised and takes less time to work with compared to RAM. You must be wondering how is the cache useful. Consider an instruction which contains a for loop to be executed 50 times. So the same instruction of the for loop will be fetched 50 times from the RAM. If the cache is there, the first time the for loop is working, the instruction will be fetched from RAM and put in the cache as well, the next 49 times that the for loop instruction has to work with will be fetched from the cache instead of the RAM. This is how the cache is useful and saves time.

The cache is smaller than RAM, expensive but faster, which instructions needs to be put in the cache and which need to be thrown out is again part of memory management.

1.2.2 Process Management

A program is a set of instructions that do some useful work. A process is a program in execution. When the program is written in the editor, it is just lines of code, when we compile the program, it becomes machine code. When we run that machine code and load it into the RAM, then it becomes a process. The CPU interacts only with RAM, whenever a program is to be executed by the CPU, it has to be brought to the RAM. The CPU will never interact with the secondary memory storage devices. If a program is saved in secondary memory storage devices, it has to be brought into the RAM, and then the CPU will execute each instruction of the machine code.

Whenever the RAM is full with the processes, the operating system decides the processes which are not currently in execution to be thrown out of the RAM so that space can be made for the ones which need execution. If a program has to be executed, it needs to be brought into the RAM. So this all is the job of the operating system to see which all processes have to be brought into the RAM and which all need to go out of the RAM. This is process management, part of the operating system's responsibilities.

In general, the operating system does the following for processes:

(a) Scheduling of processes and threads (light weight process) for the CPU

(b) Creation and deletion of both system processes as well as user processes

(c) Suspension and resumption of processes

(d) Synchronisation of processes

(e) Communication between processes

System processes are those which involve the functionalities of the operating system's job to manage and control the overall computer system whereas user processes are those which are the user made application programs that have been converted into a process (i.e. a user program in execution).

A process with a single thread has one program counter which tells from where to execute the next instruction in the sequential order when CPU is fetching an instruction from RAM.

A multi-threaded process has many program counters, each thread has its own program counter, which gives the address of the next instruction to be executed for that particular thread sequentially.

1.2.3 File Management and Input-Output Management

When the Input-Output Units are active and any transfer of data is to take place from these units, then the file manager of the operating system is responsible for handling the transfer. Suppose you want to read a file or open a file, close a file or write to a file.

Any operation involving the files will be taken care of by this manager of the operating system.

Now when we are dealing with files, then the file manager and memory manager are both active. It is not that they are isolated from each other but both managers work hand in hand to open a file or save that file on the disk.

Similarly when the program is executing, then the memory manager and process manager both work hand in hand, they do not work in isolation. But for them to work in an organised manner, the operating system is the overall in charge and makes sure that each of its managers works properly.

The input-output unit is responsible for taking the input from the keyboard and mouse and then also displaying the output on the monitor or printer, which are the output devices.

1.2.4 Security

The operating system provides security by restricting the persons who can use the system and who cannot. It does so with the help of username and password. The user is provided with a username and password, if he enters the correct username and password then the system allows him access otherwise denies it.

1.2.5 Command Interpretation

Let us first define what is command interpretation? Command Interpretation means when a user gives some commands to the system, then how does the system understand the commands and gives the desired results.

Now when we talk about command interpretation then we should know what kind of interface we should look at. The interface means whatever the user sees on the screen.

When you work in windows, where there are icons and graphics and input can be captured by mouse movements also, then it is the graphical user interface or GUI and in that when you right-click on a file, there are commands like copy, delete, rename, etc which appear on the screen.

And when you simply click on it, the operating system will work accordingly. If we do double click or single left click then the system behaves accordingly. Now if we use operating systems like DOS or UNIX, we do not have a graphical user interface.

In Command Line Interface (CLI), the input can be provided by the keyboard only and there appears a prompt (like dollar sign $ in UNIX) or in DOS, a Dos prompt like (C:\DOS>). Here you have to type a command and the system then understands it, works on it and gives the output on the screen.

For example, let us take the UNIX example, in that we give the 'pwd' command, which means print the present working directory. So the system is in whatever directory, it will print the path of the directory from the root directory. Then it will give the prompt (maybe dollar $) again on the screen so that you can enter the next command.

In Command-Line Interface you have to remember the commands and their syntax whereas in case of GUI (the command name appears on the screen, so memorising of commands is not required).

This is command interpretation, so it is the job of the operating system to understand these commands and get the job done accordingly.

1.2.6 How an Operating System Works

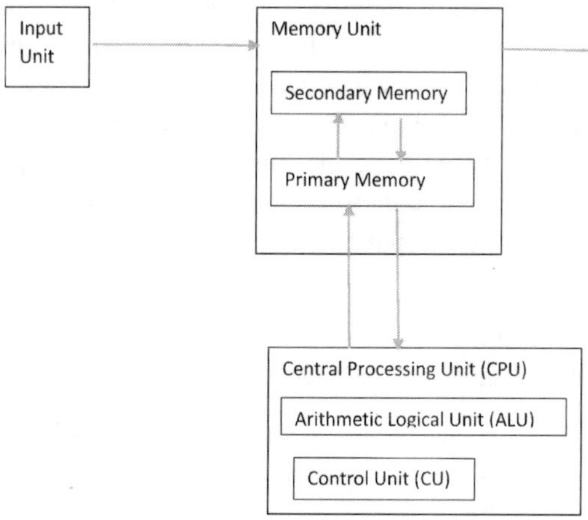

We take input from the Input Unit and produce the output on the Output Unit.

The program is saved on the secondary memory and is lying in an inactive state. Then when the program needs to be run, it is transferred from the secondary memory to primary memory, where it becomes a process. The CPU interacts only with the primary memory which is the RAM and executes the process and produces output on the output unit. Now let us see what sequence of events takes place.

Let us assume there is a small program written in C and is lying on the hard disk (C drive) in an inactive state. The C program is as follows :

```
main()
{
int a, b, c;
scanf( "%d %d", &a, &b);
c = a + b;
printf( "%d", c);
}
```

Now, this is a high-level language program which is easily readable to the user and the user can make out that we are taking two variables a and b from the input, add a and b and put the result in the variable c, then print the output c on the monitor.

First, we open the turbo C editor and open the file from the C drive. Then we compile the program (in which case it is converted into machine language instructions), then load it (in which case the machine language instructions are brought into the RAM). Then the CPU executes each instruction of the machine language (The machine language instruction form the process) and processes it, and then produces the output and prints the output on the screen. The scanf statement and the printf statement are part of the I/O management.

When the program is compiled, the machine language instructions corresponding to scanf and printf are done by the I/O.

Let us see how the CPU executes the instructions which the ALU does i.e. c = a + b

The above statement c = a + b is first converted into assembly language as follows:

LDA	R1,	A
LDA	R2,	B
ADD	R1,	R2
STR	C,	R1

Now one statement of high level language c = a + b is translated into 4 instructions of assembly language.

The instruction LDA R1, A means put the contents of the variable A into the CPU register R1.

The instruction LDA R2, B means put the contents of the variable B into the CPU register R2.

ADD R1, R2 means add the contents of register R1 and R2 and put the result into the register R1.

STR C, R1 means put the contents of register R1 (which contains a+b) into the variable C.

Now this assembly language instructions are directly converted into machine instructions (which is the binary language which the computer understands).

The LDA, ADD and STR words are called mnemonics which are directly having a set of binary digits as per the architecture of the computer.

For example, let us assume the architecture of the computer has the following:

LDA is 001100

ADD is 110011

STR is 001001

Let R1 be 110

Let R2 be 011

As per the computer system architecture of the microprocessor chip that we are using.

Let the value of variable 'A' be 1, so its binary equivalent is 001.

Let the value of variable 'B' be 2, so its binary equivalent is 010.

The variable C has value 3 (a + b) which is (1 + 2) so its binary equivalent is 3 which is 011.

Then the four assembly language instructions are translated as follows:

LDA R1, A -→ 001100 110 001

LDA R2, B -→ 001100 011 010

ADD R1, R2 -→ 110011 110 011

STR C, R1 -→ 001001 011 110

Now, this binary language is loaded into the RAM and CPU executes each instruction one by one by incrementing its program counter.

So this is how the CPU interacts only with the RAM and not with secondary memory. So all of this involves three functions of operating system i.e. (1) the I/O part which is I/O management; (2) the memory part which is memory management; and the (3) CPU part which is process management. So now the operating system is responsible for the overall coordination of all units which work hand in hand without affecting any unit or getting in any units way.

1.3 Types of Operating Systems

1.3.1 Batch Processing Operating Systems

In the olden days, the first type of an operating system came into existence, which was the batch processing operating system. It used to take several programs of the same type. These programs could be submitted together as one batch and then the user could go and do some other work while the programs in the batch were getting processed. Later on, he could come back and collect the processed results.

The programs were submitted via a punched card system, in which cards were punched with holes at different places to depict the different meaning of the input. The holes in the cards were read and the program worked accordingly. In the system, the fresh cards without any holes were kept. When the processing of the program was over, the results were given by punching holes on the fresh cards. Different holes at different places depicted different output. The interpretation of the holes on the output cards was done to obtain the results.

You can compare this with the binary code. A punched hole may depict a (1) and an unpunched hole may depict a (0). So the input and output both were given as 0's and 1's and the interpretation of this was required by the operating system.

1.3.2 Single User System

In a single-user operating system, the user is the master of the system. He issues commands to the system and the system processes each command one by one and gives back the results. The first single-user operating system was DOS (Disk Operating System) which had a Command Line Interface (CLI). A user issued one command like 'dir' on the DOS prompt, it gave the result on the screen and then the DOS prompt appeared so that the next command can be entered. The earlier version of the windows operating system was sitting on top of the DOS operating system. They had a graphical user interface and the commands could be issued through mouse clicks, but again they were simple and the operating system had to work on them at a time and produce results on the screen. The single-user Operating System was meant for personal stand-alone computers to be used at home.

Single-user Operating System may be known as an interactive operating system, which provides direct communication between the user and the system. The immediate results are expected after giving inputs by mouse or keyboard commands on the output devices. Therefore, the focus is to reduce the response time that is less than one second.

1.3.3 Multiuser Operating System

The multiuser system in contrast to single-user is that many users are sharing the resources of the computer system at the same time. Here many users are connected to a single operating system which is monitoring one high-speed CPU. So the users are sharing one CPU and one operating system. The users are connected via a network, the system where the OS resides is called a server, which serves the requests that are sent to it and the users are sitting at their terminals which are called clients. They issue their commands on the screen, the commands are sent to the operating system (on the server) which processes them and sends back the results to the individual client terminals where the command had come from. The OS uses some sort of scheduling techniques to find out which command or process will be served when.

1.3.4 Multiprogramming Operating System

The term Multiprogramming was introduced when a single program used to reside in main memory and the rest of the resources were lying idle (mainly Input/Output resources). On the other hand, when Input/Output resources were busy, the CPU was lying idle. So the designers thought that let us use a technique in which we can keep both the CPU and Input/Output resources busy at the same time to make maximum utilisation of resources and give more throughput. This design was later named as multiprogramming. For the above to happen, we would have to keep two or more programs in the active state at the same time. When one program (say P1) is using the CPU, we can make the I/O devices available to the other program (say P2). When program P1 has finished with its CPU work, we can make program P1 use the I/O devices. And when program P2 has done with I/O devices, we can make P2 use the CPU. It is not necessarily that there are only 2 programs P1 and P2. There can be more than 2, i.e. P3, P4, and P5 programs, etc. And whenever one program is using CPU, we can make another program use I/O, and when that program has done with I/O, whichever program needs CPU will get the CPU. So in this manner, the CPU can be busy most of the time by providing it to the processes that need it and I/O can be kept busy by giving I/O to programs that need it. This idea was developed because the speed of the CPU and the I/O devices had a huge difference between them and while the I/O devices were being used the CPU was lying idle most of the time.

1.3.5 Multitasking Operating System

Multitasking, on the other hand, is different from multiprogramming operating systems. In multitasking, the main memory RAM is holding several processes at the same time, whereas in Multiprogramming only one process is in the RAM using the CPU. Here more than one program is in the RAM and is getting executed simultaneously. For example, when we download a file (say process P1); play music in the background (say process P2); play a game on the screen (say process P3) at the same time. In other words when process P1, process P2 and process P3 are getting executed at the same time. That is the CPU is only one and it is giving some time to run process P1, i.e. download a file, then it pauses process P1 and gives little time to process P2 that is play the music in the background, and then it pauses process P2 and gives some time to process P3, i.e. play a game on the screen. Once one cycle is of giving time to each process is complete. It will then again start giving little, little time to each process, process P1,

Process P2 and Process P3. So in this way all 3 processes appear to work at the same time, but the fact is that they are only executing one by one by only one CPU. The difference is in the fact that CPU works in nanoseconds and human interaction or responses to the brain are in seconds. So till the time, we listen to the music or press the button of a game, the CPU has done rotation of its work on different processes P1, P2 and P3 in nanoseconds.

1.3.6 Multiprocessing Operating System

The terms Multiprogramming, Multitasking, and Multiprocessing appear similar to each other but each in its own sense has a different meaning. The first two terms have just been described, now let us turn our focus to the term multiprocessing. Multiprocessing means multiple processors or in other words multiple CPUs. When we have multiple processors, we can assign different work to different processors. They will all run in parallel and do the work assigned to them at the same time or simultaneously and the results from all of them can be collected and put together.

For example, if I have to multiply matrices and I have 4 different matrices to multiply. Now if I have one CPU or one processor then it will multiply each matrix one by one, four times. On the other hand, if I have 4 different processors or 4 different CPUs and I give each CPU one different matrix to multiply then they will work simultaneously in parallel, each one of the CPU solving one matrix multiplication at the same time and the result can then be collected from each of the 4 CPUs and put together. So the output can be produced in ¼ of the time taken by a single CPU. So this is another way of increasing the throughput of the programs.

1.3.7 Real Time Operating System

The term Real Time Operating Systems is used when we are talking of an advanced type of an operating system in which the system should be able to take the input quickly, process it at a fast speed and produce the output in fractions of a seconds time. In other words the response time should be very fast. The term response time is used to refer to the time frame between the time of submission of the job and the time it took to show the first response of the job.

This kind of system is used in automatic piloting. Automatic pilot is the term used when pilots of an aircraft want to take a break and they put the aircraft on an automatic pilot mode. So now the aircraft is handled by the computer system in which a real-time operating system is installed. It takes input from the sensors and needs to act very quickly as to how to manage if something comes in front of it. Another example of a real-time operating system is the Car Airbag in case a car meets with an accident. The airbag has to open in a definite time frame otherwise it is of no good.

There are two types of Real-Time operating systems :

(1) Soft Real-Time Operating System

(2) Hard Real-Time Operating System

In a soft real-time operating system, a little bit of flexibility is allowed in time, it has to show the response time within time limits, otherwise, if it is delayed by a few seconds, the system can still work. For example, washing machines and microwave ovens. A timer is set, they are supposed to work at that time, but if they don't nothing drastic is going to happen.

In a hard real-time operating system, no flexibility of time is allowed, if it doesn't show response time within fixed time limits then the system will fail and cannot be used as a hard real-time operating system. For example, the Car airbag in case of accident has to open immediately otherwise it is of no use, it cannot be delayed by a few seconds. Similarly, automatic piloting, delay of a few seconds may cause heavy damage since the plane is flying at extremely fast speed.

1.3.8 Distributed Operating System

The distributed operating system is again a very advanced type of an operating system. In this, the operating system is itself distributed across large geographical regions. Suppose at some region, some task of the operating system is carried out more, so that particular part of the operating system is kept at that particular location. The other part of the operating system is somewhere else. The nodes are again connected via a network and results from one place can be sent to another place and then later on collected together at one location, whichever is most suitable.

For example, at one geographical site, only the backup of each day's transactions are kept and that site is responsible for generating reports, then only that part of the operating system which is needed to generate the reports can be kept at that geographical site and this is how operating system can be distributed.

1.3.9 Time-Sharing Operating System

The Time-sharing operating system is the concept that is used in a multiuser system such as the Unix operating system. The UNIX operating system is a multiuser, multitasking and time-sharing system.

In a time-sharing system, the operating system gets several jobs or processes from many clients or user, now it has to process them all at once. So it uses a scheme in which it decides a time slice (say of 2 milliseconds). And it gives this time slice to each process one by one when the last process has had its time slice, it is again given back to the first process and the first process after doing its work in this time slice hands over the time slice to the second process and it continues until it reaches the last process again, and after the last process again it goes back to the first process in a circular manner.

It can be compared to the relay race when the stick is with one process, the person runs and hands over the stick to the next person and he runs. In this case, the stick is the time slice, when the time slice is with the process it executes for the given time slice period (say for 2 milliseconds) and then hands over the time slice to the next process which then executes and then again hands over the time slice to the third and so on. Now in this scheme, when one process has executed say for 2 milliseconds, it saves all its work done in the stack and registers, and then again when it gets the time slice after one round of completion, it will start its work from the place where it left it and get back all its work from the saved registers and stacks, and then begin executing again from the place where it had saved its work earlier, and would not have to repeat the work from the very beginning with the initial values of the variables, etc. The difference between relay race and this one is that a relay race gets over in one cycle. This continues until the processes need more time slices to complete their work. For example, if a process requires only 4 ms to complete its work then it will use 2-time slices and after the 2nd round, it will finish and thrown out of the main memory, if say a process requires 12 ms, then it requires 6 rounds of time slices and only after the 6th round it will complete its work.

And in between if a new process arrives, it will join the list at the end and time slices will be given to it also, so it will be added and get inside the loop of the time slices. So in this manner, when processes arrive they will be added to the circular list and when processes finish their work in different rounds, they will be deleted from the circular list.

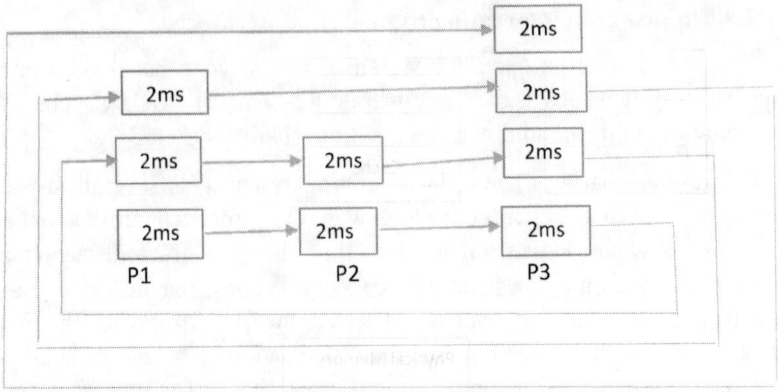

1.3.10 Types of Multiprocessing Systems

Multiprocessing systems mean there is more than one processor or CPU. The advantages of multiprocessing systems are:

(1) Increased Throughput: This means that more number of processes can be executed in the given amount of time.

(2) Economy: The cost is generally less.

(3) Increased Reliability: Which means that suppose if one processor fails. Then the other processor can keep doing the work.

There are 2 types of Multiprocessing systems:

(1) Asymmetric Multiprocessing

(2) Symmetric Multiprocessing

In Asymmetric Multiprocessing: Every processor has a particular task assigned to it. One processor is assigned the task of a master whereas the other processors are assigned the task of a slave. The processor which is the master has the control of the overall system and the slave processors wait for the master processor to give them instructions or the master processor is responsible for scheduling and assigning work to the slave processors.

In Symmetric Multiprocessing: All processors have the same status, no one is the master or no one is the slave. Every processor behaves equally. Every processor has its own set of registers and its own cache (local). But all processors share the physical memory.

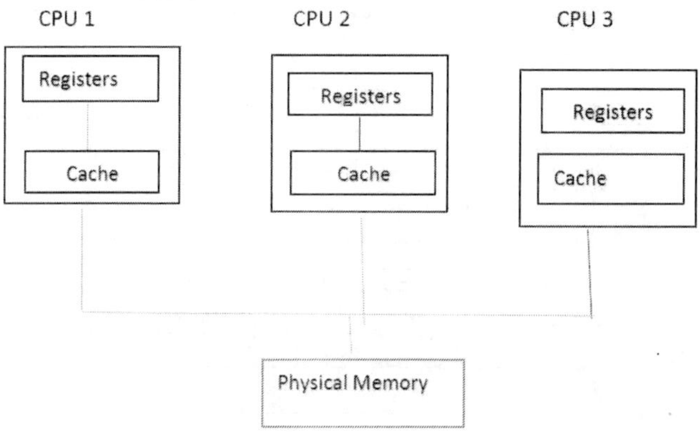

As it is clear many processors can run at the same time, sharing of data if required can be done through the same physical memory. Also in this case some CPUs may be sitting idle while the others may have a number of processes lined up in a queue to be executed. This may result in certain inefficiency. But that can be resolved by all processors working together and taking care of it by a method which will be discussed in later chapters of this book.

You must have heard of a term Dual Core. Now Dual Core means that 2 processors or CPUs are fixed together on a chip, which may look as follows:

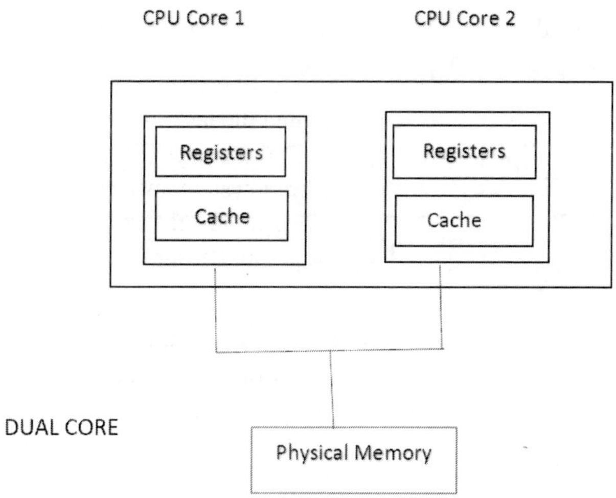

There is another term Quad Core which means 4 processors are put together on a single chip.

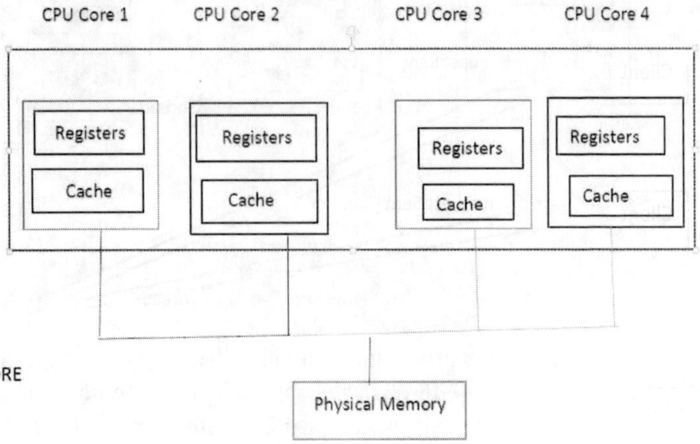

QUAD CORE

1.3.11 Multithreading Systems

A process may contain a number of threads. A thread is a light weight process. The difference between thread and process is that process is formed from a program whereas the threads are formed from a process. The threads therefore can share code, data and files which need not be written again and again for the same process they belong to.

Although a thread has its own:

(1) Thread Id

(2) Program Counter

(3) Register Stack

(4) Stack

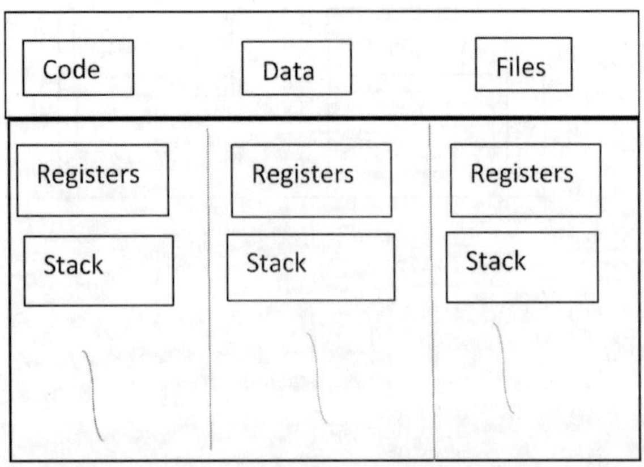

To take an example of multithreading process, let us take an example of a client-server architecture. In client server architecture, there is one server which processes the requests from various clients.

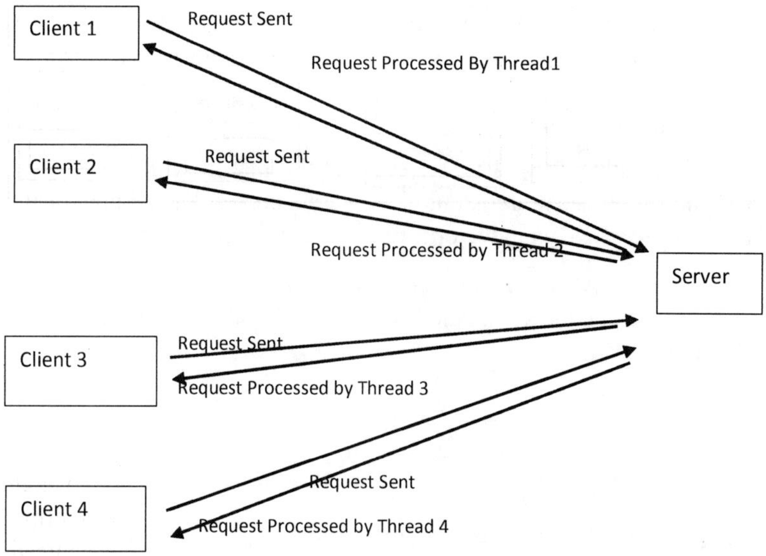

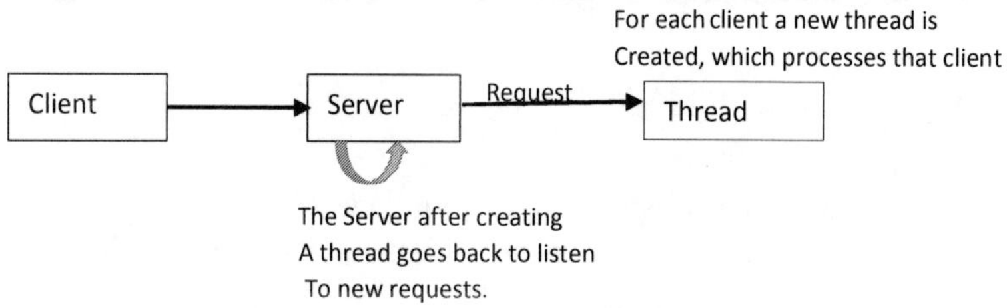

Now in this architecture, it can clearly be seen that clients send requests to, it can clearly be seen that clients send requests at the same time or one after another. If the server itself starts processing the first request sent by a client, the other client requests will be kept pending. So what does the server do? It creates a thread for the first request and that thread then takes over to process the request from the client. The server is then free and goes back to listen to further requests from clients. So when another request from another client comes, it creates another thread and that thread then does the processing. So the server is never busy processing any request, it is always only busy creating threads and listening to requests sent by the clients.

1.4 Operating System Structure

The operating system structure defines how an operating system is organised to perform the various functions that are allocated to it.

1.4.1 Monolithic Kernel

A Monolithic Kernel architecture is the one in which the whole operating system software is put in the kernel area. A Kernel is basically the area which is given to the operating system software.

There are two modes in this architecture, the user mode (in which the user operates) and the kernel mode (in which the whole operating system software is placed).

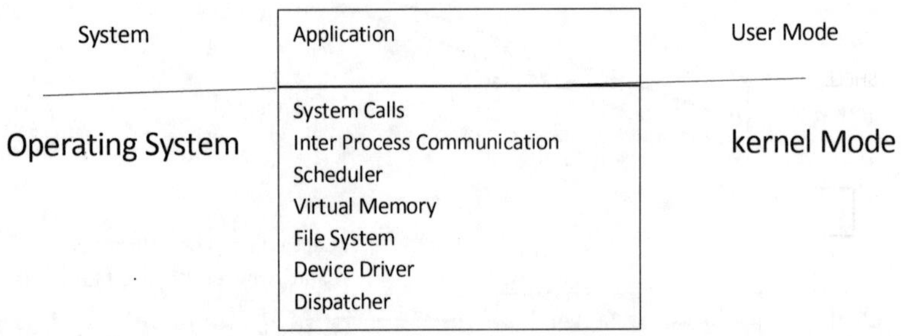

The kernel mode is also the supervisor mode, UNIX operating system known as the Unix Kernel is an example of a monolithic kernel architecture.

Other examples that follow are:

LINUX Operating System and MS-DOS (Disk Operating System) which use the monolithic architecture.

In this type, there is only one address space. All the operating system services exist and execute in this address space.

1.4.2 Layered Operating System Architecture

In this architecture the system is divided into 4 layers:

(1) The Hardware Layer

(2) The Kernel Layer

(3) The Shell Layer
(4) The User Layer

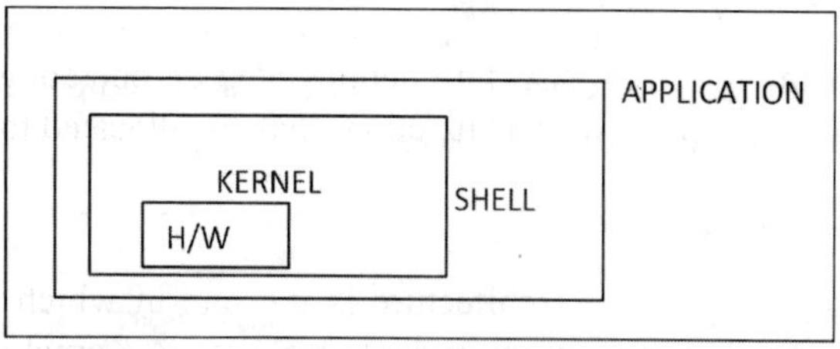

The innermost layer is the H/W Layer, on top of that is the Kernel Layer (which consists of operating system routines). On top of that is the Shell Layer. And the outermost layer is where the User is residing.

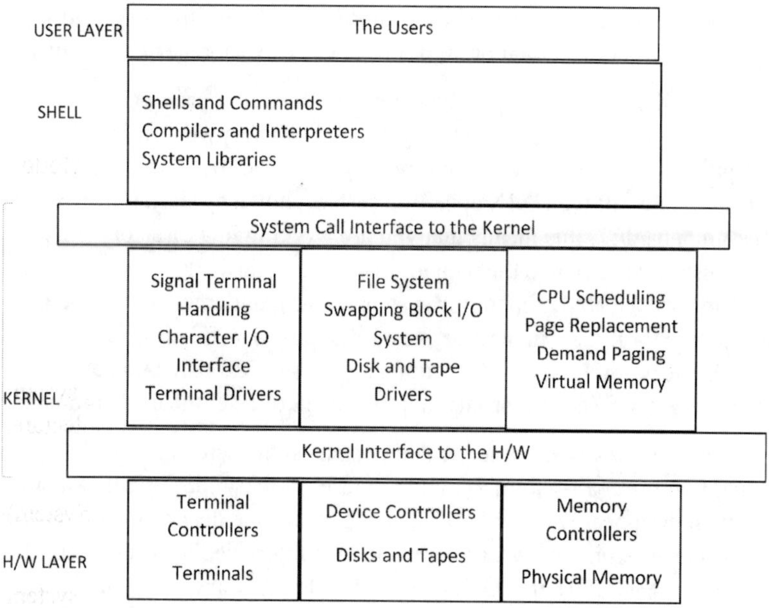

The above diagram shows the components of each layer.

The Shell basically provides the interface where the user can write his commands and instruct the operating System to do some work.

There are 2 types of user interfaces, one is the Command Line Interface (CLI), the other is the Graphical User Interfaces (GUI). What you find in

DOS operating system or the UNIX operating system is the Command Line Interface, where the shell appears on the screen and you can type your commands on the prompt provided by the shell and execute programs.

In case of the UNIX shell, there is a $ (dollar) prompt or a # (hash) prompt depending upon the type of shell we are using. Similarly, the UNIX system uses Command Line Interfaces.

```
$ ls
....
....
$
```

Figure 1

```
$ pwd
/usr/archana/dir1
$
```

Figure 2

Consider Figure 1, suppose we give commands like 'ls' (which is the equivalent of the 'dir' command in DOS), which gives the list of current directories and files present in the present working directory, and then appears with another dollar prompt, so that you can enter the next command.

Consider Figure 2, suppose we give on the dollar prompt a command 'pwd' (which means present working directory). The 'pwd' commands gives the path of the present working directory from the root (which is the top most directory of the UNIX operating system shown by slash (/). So it says /usr/archana/dir1, this means that you are working in a directory 'dir1' at the present moment and the path to 'dir1' is as follows. From the top most directory of the UNIX operating system (root /), underneath the root there lies a directory 'usr', underneath 'usr' is 'archana' and below 'archana' is the directory 'dir1'. Once the command has been executed, the answer is shown and the $ (dollar) prompt appears again to enter the next command.

In GUI Interface, the icons that appear on the screen is the shell and when you press a right click by the mouse on the folder or file, a list of commands appear which when clicked, perform the desired operation. So this is the difference between Command Line Interface (CLI) and Graphical user Interface (GUI), that GUI is more user friendly and you don't have to remember any of the commands, they just get executed without typing simply clicking on them (such as copy, cut, rename, delete, paste etc.)

Now let us return to our layered architecture. In this case, the upper level layer can invoke operations on the lower level layer, or the higher level layer can call the routines in the lower level layer. The advantage of this type of architecture is that it is simple to build and easy to debug.

The layers use functions or operations or services of only the layers that belong below them.

There are certain disadvantages with this architecture and they are mainly two:

(1) Because upper level layers can call only lower level layers, the plan of the architecture should be done very carefully.

(2) The layered architecture is less efficient in terms of throughput.

Let us take the first disadvantage and explain it.

Suppose we have a multiprogramming environment. In Multiprogramming the CPU and the I/O need to work in parallel in order to keep the CPU busy most of the time. So in that case, the I/O operations backing store or physical memory are at a layer above the CPU layer. While the program is waiting to do some I/O. The CPU can do some rescheduling of its processes. So the CPU layer is below the I/O layer.

Now let us take the case of Virtual Memory. Virtual Memory means that RAM is the Primary Memory and because RAM's capacity is limited and programs may require to bring in their pages into the RAM, from the disk, and the programs which have been executed by the CPU and no longer require the CPU may be brought out of the RAM and put on disk, so in this case the disk acts as a virtual memory (which is, it is not real, but appears that everything is working with the RAM only). Now the CPU scheduler will be having all the information about which processes are active and need to fit in the memory. So that the CPU can swap in / swap out the processes onto the memory. So the CPU needs to be in the upper layer and the Physical Memory which requires I/O needs to be below the CPU layer.

So in such a case problems will arise to put which part on top and which at the bottom concerning the CPU and the I/O.

The second disadvantage is that there is a lot of overhead involved in passing data from one layer to another, in which case it makes the system less efficient.

To explain this further, let us define a term system call. For example, let us assume that a user program executes an I/O operation. Now the program executes a system call that is stuck in the I/O layer. This may in turn call the memory management layer, which in turn calls the CPU scheduling layer and finally it passes to the H/W layer.

At each layer parameters have to be changed, and data has to be passed. There are system calls in between layers which need to be invoked and these system calls in turn take a lot more time than is required.

1.4.3 System Calls

A system call is the routine written in C or C++ inside the operating system or the kernel which provide the actual services to do some task. The system call uses an interface called the Application Programmers Interface (API) between the user mode and the kernel mode.

The user's program contain a function, which is passed through the system call interface to invoke the system call written inside the kernel.

For example, let us take the open() function to open a file in a C program. Now the user's program will contain an open function which is a standard function defined in a standard header file say stdio.h. The open function will use the system call interface to call the system call open, which is written inside the kernel, or is written as part of the operating system routine to do the necessary work associated in opening a file. This is explained diagrammatically as follows:

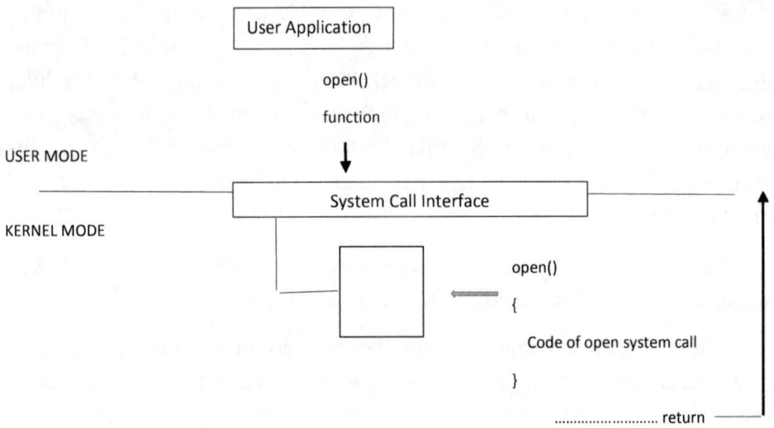

1.4.4 Microkernels

The microkernel as the name suggests is a small kernel. Small kernel or small operating system means that only those services of the operating system will be kept in the kernel which are necessary and required to be kept in the kernel. The services which are not necessary to be kept in the kernel are kept in the user space as application programs or system programs.

It is very important to find out which services should be kept in the kernel space and which should be moved to the user space. The microkernel acts as an interface and provides communication between the user space services and the client program or the application program written by the client. The communication is done through message passing. Message passing is a communication technique which is discussed later on in this book.

The client program does not interact with the server directly, it has to go through the operating system, which is either the microkernel or the user space services. For example, if a client needs to access a file, it must interact with the file server.

The advantage with microkernel is that it can be extended, to the extent that all new services can be put into the user space and later on (these services) will not require to change the microkernel. They will do all the necessary changes in the user space.

Microkernel can be ported from one h/w to another because of its design, that it is small in nature.

The microkernel also provides more security and reliability. This is due to the fact that most of the services of the operating system are running in the user space rather than the kernel space. So if one gets affected or corrupted, the others don't stop working and the microkernel is also doing its work. While the other services are working the one which was affected can be repaired.

Let us see, which are the services which are kept in user space and which are the ones which are kept in kernel space.

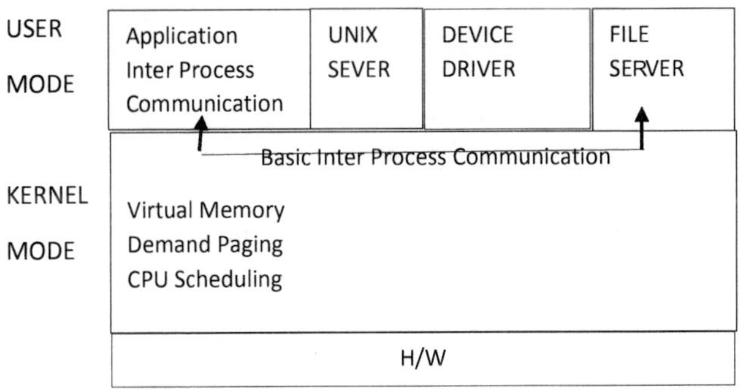

The Application Inter Process Communication needs to contact the File Server, then it has to go through the microkernel.

1.4.5 Re-Entrant Kernel

In normal case, an operating system works as follows, that when a service request comes, the user mode process is suspended which in turn calls the system call in the kernel mode, the kernel thread executes and then the kernel mode is also suspended (or the kernel is blocked). By suspended we mean the user process or kernel process cannot do any other task, and they are executing only one process at one time.

What is different in the re-entrant kernel is that the kernel can be re-entered. Just like we have multiple threads at the user level (which means multiple processes can be run at the same time in the user mode). Similarly the kernel mode has multiple threads in kernel mode in an re-entrant kernel. This means that the kernel mode is not blocked by one process running in kernel mode, there can be multiple threads working simultaneously in the kernel mode also and that is why the name re-entrant kernel, which means that the kernel can be re-entered again. Once one thread is executing in the kernel mode, other threads can also run simultaneously in the kernel mode.

The kernel threads share the same memory. In re-entrant kernel, the CPU can do any other task, while one thread is running. The other processes are not stopped from entering the kernel mode.

Let us take an example of an I/O wait. Suppose a process wants to read a file, in that case, it will call the system call or the kernel function to read a file.

Suppose inside the kernel function, the disk controller asks for some data. To get the data, some time is required, in that case, the function for that file read is blocked.

So, now in the case of re-entrant kernel, the scheduler will assign the CPU to another kernel thread, requiring some kernel function. When the data has come and is ready for the read file function, the interrupt will come and the kernel is ready to execute the read file function again, so that kernel thread of read file function will be resumed from where it stopped and in this way the kernel does not get blocked by one kernel thread, but multiple threads of kernel can be executed by scheduling them properly.

1.5 Operating System Components

The essential part of the operating system resides in the RAM, the rest of the operating system is kept on the disk. Similarly all the processes that are ready to run are kept in the RAM simultaneously.

OS
JOB 1
JOB 2
JOB 3
JOB 4

The main ability of the operating system is to multiprogram. It is not possible for a single process to keep the CPU busy and the I/O busy at the same time.

Generally multiple programs kept in the RAM are programs which are running at the same time. It is just that they are alternating between the CPU and the I/O.

The advantage of multiprogramming is that it increases CPU utilisation by organising jobs (which consists of code and data). So that the CPU is having always some process to executes.

The operating system keeps many jobs in the memory simultaneously. Since the RAM is small enough to accommodate all jobs, the rest are kept on the disk in the job pool. The job pool on the disk is waiting to get some space in the main memory i.e., the RAM. The jobs that are kept in the memory i.e. RAM are alternating the CPU and the I/O.

When a job has finished execution, it is taken out of the RAM and put back in the job pool on disk. When a process needs to execute, it is taken from the disk job pool and brought into the RAM.

1.6 Operating System Services

The operating system services can be divided into 2 categories:

(a) Services that provide functions that are helpful to the user.

(b) Services that make sure that the system itself is running its operations efficiently.

(a) The first category consists of the following services which are helpful for the user:

   (1) User Interface

(2) Program Execution
(3) I/O Operations
(4) File system manipulation
(5) Communication
(6) Error Detection

(b) The second category consists of the following which the system does for itself:
(1) Resource Allocation
(2) Accounting
(3) Protection and Security

(a) Services Helpful For the User:

(1) User Interface:

The user interface means that the interface between the user and the operating system. So between the user and the operating system is the screen which is either Command Line Interface (CLI) like UNIX and DOS or Graphical User Interface (GUI), like WINDOWS.

The user interface should be designed in a manner that is user friendly, and easy to operate for the user, with the help of the user interface, the user will be able to use the operating system.

As it was discussed earlier, in Command Line Interface (CLI), you have to remember the names of the commands and their syntax, whereas in Graphical User Interface (GUI). It is easy to use, operate and no need to remember any commands or syntax.

(2) Program Execution:

The Operating System should be able to load a program in memory i.e. the RAM and run it.

(3) I/O Operations:

The Operating System should be able to work with Input/Output Units and files, and may be able to do I/O wait operations and work effectively by alternating between the I/O and CPU in proper coordination to do multiprogramming.

(4) File System Manipulation:

The operating system should be able to

(1) Create a File
(2) Delete a File

(3) Modify a File
(4) Read a File
(5) Write to a File
(6) Search a File
(7) List the files in a directory

Some files also allow permissions management, which means to allow or deny access to files and directories based upon the fact that who is the owner of the files.

For example, in UNIX operating system we have a file's listing as

-rwxr-x—x file1.c

As you can see the starting dash sign (-) indicates that it is a file, then are given the permissions. The first 3 (rwx) in this case is for the owner of the file. The next 3 (r-x) in this case is for the group and the last 3 (—x) in this case are for others.

Suppose there is a C program stored in a file named file1.c . Now suppose there is a student who is the owner of the file, so in the above case he has all the 3 permissions (rwx), to read, write and execute the file. Suppose this student is working on a project and his group members are given the permission to read his file and execute it, so that they can take help from the code and also test the code, but they cannot write to his file so that the file is not modified, so as in the above case they are given the permissions to read and execute and not write(r-x). Now the rest of the class cannot either read the file or write to it, but they can just execute the file to see that the program is working. So they are not given the read and the write permissions, only the permission to execute, so as in above case it is (—x).

Chapter - 2

Process Synchronisation

2.1 Introduction to Concurrent Processes

Processes that run concurrently mean that two processes are running simultaneously in the memory which can further be described as follows:

Suppose there are 2 processes P1 and P2. If we talk of serial execution, then first process P1 executes and finishes then process P2 executes and finishes, there is no interference between them as shown in the diagram below:

P1 P2

--------- --------

Or vice versa that process P2 executes first and finishes, then process P1 executes and finishes. so the diagram looks as follows:

P1 P2

--------- --------

Now concurrent processes on the other hand mean that some part of process P1 executes, then it stops, then some part of process P2 executes, then it halts, then process P1 starts to execute again from where it stopped and so on.

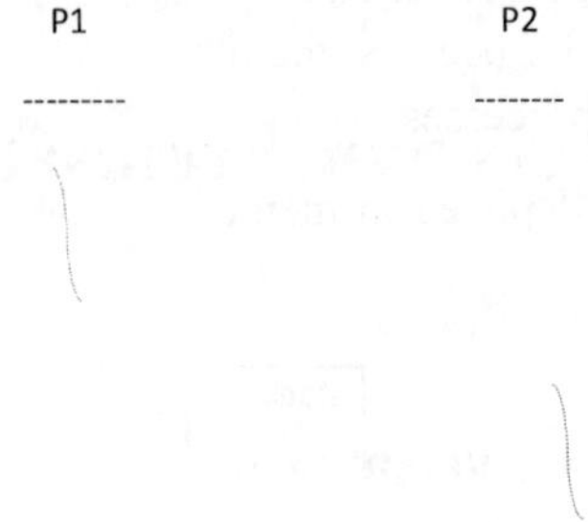

Concurrent processes may share the address space which contains code and data. This happens generally in the case where threads are used.

There are other ways also in which data can be shared among concurrent processes and that is through files and messages. When the data shared in read only mode, then there is no problem but when shared data becomes a Read / Write operation, then it may lead to inconsistent data. If the processes run serially, then the data inconsistency still holds, but in case of concurrent processes, the data inconsistency problem arises.

As we all know, a process is a program in execution and also a process is a unit of work in time sharing systems.

There are a number of processes which might be working together in synchronized manner:

(1) Operating System Processes
(2) Executing System Code
(3) User Processes which execute user code.

2.2 The Concept of a Process

A job, process and task generally refer to the same term which is a process. In Batch Processing operating systems, we used the term job for a process. In a time shared system, we use the term tasks or user processes. In a stand alone PC, there may be a number of programs running simultaneously. For example:

(1) A Web Browser

(2) An Email Package

(3) An Excel Sheet

Even if the system is running only one program, it may need to do certain activities to keep track of how the memory is to be managed. These internal activities which are required to manage the memory are also tasks. And these tasks are also processes, the difference is that they are system processes and not user processes.

A process may be depicted in memory (RAM) with the help of the following diagram:

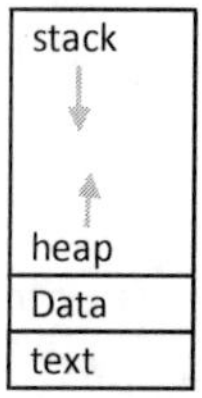

The code of the program lies in the text section. This program code is nothing, but the instructions which are in machine language, the executable file. The program counter tells you which instruction is to be executed from the text section. The data section mainly consists of the global variables of the program. The process stack includes the return addresses of the functions called, local variables inside main or any other function and also the parameters passed to the functions. The heap is used for dynamic memory allocation i.e. when we call the calloc or malloc function and storage is required from memory then this memory is given from the heap space. So this memory is given dynamically at run time.

The heap and the stack grow towards each other and the space between them is empty, because we do not know how much space the stack and the heap will require, because the stack may shrink or grow as and when the functions come and go. Similarly the dynamic memory may be asked for and released at run time. It is only that the text and the data sections are fixed, because we know of their length.

2.3 The Principle of Concurrency

The principle of concurrency needs to be followed by the concurrent processes, so that they work in synchronisation and it states that:

(1) It looks to the processes as if they are the only ones which are occupying the machine. But the fact is that they are all running.

(2) It appears as if they are executing serially, so that there are no conflicts arising among them.

(3) They follow the principle of mutual exclusion. Mutually exclusive processes are those, which allow only one process to run, and if that process is running, the others are not running. When any other process starts to run, then all other processes are not running at that time.

(4) The memory segment between the processes is a shared one. But no process overwrites whatever has been written onto it by another process previously.

2.4 The Producer-Consumer Problem

There are two entities, one a producer which produces some item, another a consumer which consumes the item produced earlier by the producer. For example, a server is a producer and the client is the consumer. In this let us assume that there is a web server which produces some image files and the clients are the consumers which with the help of their web browsers request for those image files and then take them.

The producer-consumer problem can be solved with the help of the shared memory segment.

The Producers and Consumers are also running concurrently, so there needs to be a buffer where the producer after producing the items can place them and the consumer simultaneously can use that buffer to extract the items produced, so that it can consume them.

The buffer naturally lies in an area of memory that is shared both by the producer and the consumer processes.

A producer produces an item, and simultaneously the consumer can consume another item. Both the producer and the consumer need to be synchronized so that the consumer does not consume an item, which has not yet been produced by the producer.

The buffer where both processes place their items is bounded (which means it has a definite fixed size) and is not of an unlimited capacity.

So now the producer and the consumer have to face another challenge. If the buffer is empty, i.e. there are no items in the buffer at the moment, so the consumer needs to wait, because it cannot consume anything. The buffer may be empty because of two reasons: (1) It is an initial condition, where producer has not yet started producing anything or (2) the consumer has consumed all the items which producer produced. So now it is waiting for the producer to produce something first, so that the consumer can consume it.

If the buffer is full, then the producer has to wait. Because if the producer is fast enough in producing items, and consumer is slow enough of consuming them, then the buffer does not have any new place to put its newly produced items in the buffer. Since it is a fixed size buffer and it is full, so the producer has to wait till the consumer consumes some items and makes an empty slot in the buffer.

Now let us write the code:

```
    #define BUFFER_LENGTH 10
    typedef struct{
            ....
            } item;
item buffer[BUFFER_LENGTH];
int enter =0;
int exit = 0;
```

The shared buffer behaves like a circular array of items with 2 pointers 'enter' and 'exit' to indicate the positions from where we can enter into the buffer to place an item, and from where we can enter into the buffer to place an item, and from where we can exit to consume an item.

The variable 'enter' is pointing to the next position in the buffer, which is free. The variable 'exit' is pointing to the first full position of the buffer.

The buffer is empty when both

(1) 'enter' and 'exit' have a value 0. (initial condition).

(2) when enter == exit, i.e. when producer produced items and consumer consumed all of them, so again the buffer is empty, but it can be at any position in the buffer.

The buffer is full when (enter +1) % BUFFER_LENGTH == exit

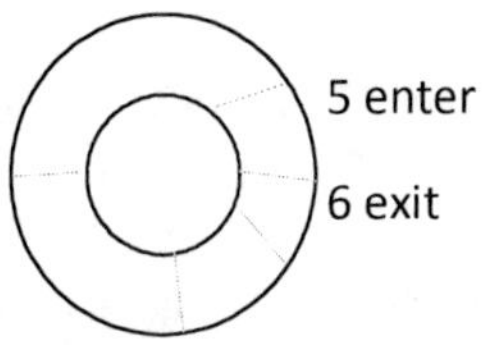

Let us look at how the above condition is satisfied. Suppose initially, when the buffer was empty, enter and exit were both initialised to zero. Now producer started producing items and went ahead by increasing the enter pointer. The consumer also started consuming items and moved ahead the exit pointer. Suppose the exit pointer was at a position 6 in the buffer length of 10. Now producer reached to the position 9 and saw that the consumer had consumed items from position 0 to 5 and so the slots from 0 to 5 were empty. So producer produced more items and filled the slots from 0 to 5. Now the enter pointer moved to the position 5. And the pointer is at position no. 6. So the buffer is full, so when the enter pointer is one position less than the exit pointer, then the buffer is full. Therefore,

(enter + 1) % BUFFER_LENGTH == exit

or

(5 + 1) % 10 == 6

6 % 10 == 6

6 == 6

Now let us write the code of the producer and the consumer processes. The producer process has a local variable 'produceditem', in which it stores the newly produced item. The consumer process has a local variable 'consumeditem' in which it stores the item to be consumed.

The producer code

```
item  produceditem;
while (true) {
      /* produce an item in produceditem */
      while (( (enter + 1)%BUFFER_LENGTH) == exit)
            ; /* do nothing */
      buffer[enter] = produceditem;
      enter = (enter + 1)%BUFFER_LENGTH ;
}
```

In the above producer code, the produceditem is an item which the producer has just produced and it wants to put this produceditem into the buffer. So it runs in an infinite loop, keep checking for the condition that whether the buffer is full or not. If it finds that the buffer is full, so it does nothing, just keeps repeating in the while loop. If when ever it finds an empty slot, then the condition that the buffer is full will not be true, it will put at the pointer position 'enter', the newly produced item in the buffer and increment the 'enter' logical pointer by 1. So that the enter logical pointer now shows the next empty slot where the producer can put its next newly produceditem.

There is a similar code for the consumer process.

The consumer code

```
item consumeditem;
while (true) {
while (enter == exit)
; //do nothing
consumeditem = buffer[exit];
exit = (exit + 1) %BUFFER_LENGTH ;
/* consume the item in the consumeditem variable */
}
```

In the above consumer code, the consumeditem is a variable in which the consumer code will extract the item from the buffer and put it inside that variable. Remember that the consumer code cannot consume anything if the buffer is empty. So it keeps on checking the empty condition endlessly in a while loop. If the buffer is empty it does nothing, just keeps rotating in the while loop. As soon as it finds that the buffer is no longer empty and there are items that can be consumed. It extracts the item from the buffer where the pointer exit is pointing, puts it in the variable consumeditem and increments the logical pointer exit by 1 so that the consumer can extract the next item from that position.

The above producer and consumer codes have the problem that the length of the buffer is fixed, and it works only in the cases where the no. of items are BUFFER_LENGTH -1 at the same time.

If we want to remove the above deficiency, we will have to modify the code. One way of doing that is to have a variable called count initialised to 0. We will increment count whenever the producer produces an item in the buffer and decrement count whenever the consumer consumes an item from the buffer. So, in this case, we will be able to work with more number of items at the same time.

The producer modified code

```
while (true) {
    /* produce an item in produced item */
    while (count == BUFFER_LENGTH)
    ; //do nothing
    buffer[enter] = produceditem;
    enter = (enter + 1) %BUFFER_LENGTH;
    count++;
    }
```

The consumer modified code

```
while (true) {
    while (count == 0 )
    ; //do nothing
    consumeditem = buffer[exit];
    exit = (exit + 1) % BUFFER_LENGTH ;
    count —;
    /* consume the item in the consumed item variable*/
    }
```

The above modified producer and modified consumer code will work well when executed separately. But if they are executed at the same time, they will not work correctly because they are working on the same variable count. Let us take an example to explain this:

Suppose the value of the count variable is 7. And since the producer modified code and consumer modified code execute concurrently, so they both execute the statements count++ and count— concurrently.

The value of the count variable may be 6, 7 or 8 depending upon the order of execution of statements. Ideally if both statements count++ and count— have been executed, then in whichever order they are executed, the value of the count variable should remain 7, which was the original value. Suppose count++ happens first and then count— happens. So the value of count goes from 7 to 8 and then back to 7.

Suppose now count— happens first and then count++ happens. So the value of count should go from 7 to 6 and then to 7. How is it possible that it gives us a value 6 or 8 of the count variable out of which none is correct. Let us see how this happens:

Suppose count++ may be implemented on a machine language (on a typical machine) as :

T1: Register1 = count

T2: Register1 = Register1 +1

T3: count = Register1

Where Register1 may be one of the local CPU registers. The statements count—may be implemented as follows in the same machine language:

T4: Register2 = count

T5: Register2 = Register2 -1

T6: count = Register2

Now T1, T2, T3 and T4, T5, T6 are running concurrently and can occur in any order. Suppose the order of execution is as follows:

T1: Register1 = count	(Value of Register1 is 7)
T2: Register1 = Register1 +1	(Value of Register1 is 8)
T4: Register2 = count	(Value of Register2 is 7)
T5: Register2 = Register2 -1	(Value of Register2 is 6)
T3: count = Register1	(Value of count is 8)
T6: count = Register2	(Value of count is 6)

So finally count got the value of 6.

Suppose the order of execution of the above statements was as follows:

T1: Register1 = count	(Value of Register1 is 7)
T2: Register1 = Register1 +1	(Value of Register1 is 8)
T4: Register2 = count	(Value of Register2 is 7)
T5: Register2 = Register2 -1	(Value of Register2 is 6)
T6: count = Register2	(Value of count is 6)
T3: count = Register1	(Value of count is 8)

So finally count got the value of 8.

This problem is occurring because we are allowing both processes producer and consumer to manipulate the same variable count at the same time or concurrently.

In both cases, whichever register writes last to the count variable, its value is taken, and the one above it, its value is overwritten. This leads to race condition, which means when several processes are manipulating the variable concurrently and the outcome depends on the order of execution of the statements. Then they are competing to write last.

To avoid Race condition, we will have to make sure that only one process at a time

Is manipulating the variable count. This forms the basis for process synchronisation and co-ordination.

2.5 The Critical - Section Problem

Suppose in a system, there are a number of processes (n) ranging from { P0, P1,….Pn-1}.

Each of the process has its own segment of code, which is called the critical section. In this critical section the processes may do the following:

(a) Update Common Variables

(b) Update Tables

(c) Write to a file

When a process enters its own critical section, no other process is allowed to enter its critical section. Remember every process has its own critical section. This means no 2 processes execute their critical section at the same time.

The critical section problem addresses the fact that the processes executing must co-operate.

To co-operate means that:

(1) Each process must first make a request to enter its critical section.

(2) This request is made in the section of code which is called the entry section.

(3) Then when request is granted, the process enters its critical section. This section of code is called the critical section.

(4) Then when the process leaves its critical section. It must tell other processes that it is leaving. So this section of code is called the exit section.

(5) The critical section may be followed by the piece of code of the process which is not critical. And this section of code is called the remainder section.

So, the general structure of any process would look like this:

```
do {
        | Entry Section |
                            Critical Section
        | Exit Section  |
                            Remainder Section
} while (true);
```

The processes, which enter their critical section must satisfy the following 3 processes:

(1) Mutual Exclusion: If one process P1 is executing in its critical section, then no other processes can execute their critical sections. That is, they should be mutually exclusive. If one is executing the critical section, then the others have to wait until that process stops executing its critical section. And then other processes can enter their critical section. Again when another process will enter its critical section, all other processes will be waiting for their turn.

(2) Progress: If no process is executing in its critical section. And a number of processes are lined up to enter their critical sections. Then only those processes which are not executing their remainder sections will be allowed to participate in deciding which one will enter the critical section. This is because of the fact that any process which is executing its remainder section means that, it has just left its critical section and is now in its remainder section. So that process is not given a chance to enter the critical section again. The others which have been waiting must be given the chance to enter their critical sections, so they make the decisions.

(3) Bounded Waiting: There exists a limit on the no. of times that other processes get a chance to enter their critical sections, after a process has made a request to enter its critical section and before that request is granted. This is to take care of the fact that if one process is given the chance to enter its critical section again and again, so other processes will keep on waiting endlessly and they may never get their chance. So there has to be a limit on the number of times a process can execute its critical section depending on the number of requests made.

There are 2 ways to handle critical sections by the operating systems:

(1) Pre-emptive Kernel

(2) Non Pre-emptive kernel

Pre-emption means that a task can be stopped while it is running, i.e. it can be suspended for some time and then resume later on from where it had left its work.

A pre-emptive kernel allows a process to stop it or interrupt it while it is running in kernel mode.

A non pre-emptive kernel does not allow a process which is running in kernel mode to be stopped in the middle. Here the kernel will finish whatever task it is doing and no process can interrupt it in the middle.

A non pre-emptive kernel does not face the problem of race condition because it is active at a single task at a time. It will finish whatever has been assigned to it before taking up any other task.

A pre-emptive kernel may face the problem of race conditions. So it needs to be designed carefully. A pre-emptive kernel is used where real-time programming is involved, so that processes in real time can pre-empt the kernel to sop the process which is executing and do the other higher priority processes whenever they require to pre-empt the kernel.

The pre-emptive kernel also seems to be more responsive which means that whatever inputs are given to it, it takes care of them and responds in time to other processes so that no process is waiting for a long period of time to get its turn for execution.

2.5.1 Peterson's Solution

To solve the critical section problems, a number of solutions have come up. One of them is a s/w based solution known as the Peterson's Solution.

Peterson's solution works only between two processes. When one process is working in its critical section, the second works in the remainder section and when the second is working in its critical section, the first works in its remainder section.

The processes are numbered P0 and P1. They can also be labelled as Pi and Pj,

such that j = 1–i

Peterson's solution requires that the processes should be sharing the following data items, one a vriable and another an array as follows:

```
int turn;
boolean flag[2];
```

The variable 'turn' indicates whose turn it is to enter its critical section. The array 'flag' indicates whether a process is ready to enter its critical section or not.

If turn == i, then the process Pi is allowed to enter its critical section. To enter the critical section for a process Pi, it should be ready, so in that case the flag[i] will be true and it should be allowed also. So to be allowed, the turn should be equal to i. (turn == i).

A process works as follows to enter its critical section. The process Pi first sets flag[i] to be true and sets turn = j . (i.e. it gives the other process the chance to enter its critical section. The variable turn is set by the operating system, giving that process the chance to enter its critical section. Suppose turn is set to i, then i will enter its critical section. If turn is set to j, then j will enter its critical section. If turn i and j are both set at the same time, then the statement which executed last will be taken care of and the one which was written just previously will be overwritten and not taken into consideration. Suppose the order of statements occur as follows:-

```
turn = i;
turn = j;
```

then j will enter the critical section and turn = i is overwritten by turn =j;

If the order of execution is as follows:

```
turn = j;
turn = i;
```

then i will enter the critical section and turn = j is overwritten by turn =i;

Consider the following piece of code for process Pi.

```
do {
    flag[i] = TRUE;
    turn = j;
    while (flag[j] && turn ==j)
            ; //do nothing
            Critical Section
```

```
        flag[i] = FALSE; //exit condition
                Remainder Section
    } while (TRUE);
```

Now in process Pi, it has set flag[i] = TRUE, so this process Pi is ready to enter its critical section and it has set turn = j. So it says, that if the other process (Pj) wants to enter its critical section, it can do so.

The statements { while (flag[j] && turn == j) } means that Pj is ready to enter its critical section (flag[j] ==TRUE) and the variable turn is also set to j (j is allowed). So this condition indicates that j is ready as well as allowed to enter its critical section, or Pj is in its critical section. So the process Pi has to wait, that is why Pi is executing do nothing (because both the conditions (ready and allowed) are in favour of Pj to be in its critical section). Now when Pj will leave its critical section, it will set flag[j] = FALSE (Pj's part of the exit condition). So now the while condition will no longer be true. Now flag[i] is already set to true in Pi, as soon as the operating system sets the variable turn == i, that is the operating system gives process Pi a chance to enter its critical section, Pi will do so and when process Pi wants to indicate that it has finished its critical section, it will do so by making the flag[i] = False (Pi's part of the exit condition).

The code for process Pj is as follows:

```
do {
    flag[j] = TRUE;
    turn = i;
    while (flag[i] && turn ==i )
            ; //do nothing
            Critical Section
    flag[j] = FALSE;            //exit condition
            Remainder Section
} while (true);
```

So here you can see that when flag[i] was true and turn == i, then process Pi was executing its critical section and process Pj was doing nothing. As soon as Pi indicated to leave its critical section, it set flag[i] = FALSE (Pi's exit condition). And the while condition in Pj was no longer TRUE, so Pj must have entered its critical section.

Both processes cannot be in their critical section at the same time, because the ready condition says that flag[i] == flag[j] == TRUE at the same time. And to be allowed to enter the critical section, turn should be equal to i or should be equal to j. So turn cannot be 0 or 1 critical section. If it is 1 that means Pj or P1 will be in its critical section.

2.5.2 Test and Set Instruction

Test and set is another s/w based solution which is using locks to enter the critical section and unlock to exit the critical section.

The structure of the code is as follows:

```
do {
    | Acquire Lock |
                        Critical Section
    | Release Lock |
                        Remainder Section
} while (true);
```

Test and Set is based on the fact as its name suggests that we test the instruction first and set the lock on it automatically. (All processes access the same variable 'lock')

If there are 2 machines (CPUs) and they are both executing test and set instruction, then they will be executed in some serial order and will follow the principle of mutual exclusion, so no 2 processes enter their critical section at the same time.

The code of the instruction is as follows:

```
boolean TestandSet (boolean *target)
{
    boolean returnvalue = *target;
    *target = TRUE;
    return returnvalue;
}
```

The code for the process Pi is as follows:

```
do {
    while (TestandSet (&lock) )
```

```
            ; //do nothing
            Critical Section
      lock = FALSE;          //exit condition
            Remainder Section
  } while (true);
```

Now the process Pi calls the TestandSet function with the value of a boolean pointer variable 'lock'. The lock is initially initialised to false.

Now if Pi wants to enter its critical section, it will call Testand Set (& lock) with lock variable which is initialised to false. The 'lock' variable is received in TestandSet by a pointer variable 'target'. A local Boolean variable 'returnvalue' stores what was passed to it from target, that is returnvalue = false. The contents of the target variable are set to true, so from the calling function Pi, the lock variable is set to true. And the TestandSet Instruction returns the returnvalue variable which was set to false. So from the calling process Pi, now the value of the variable lock has been set to true and the while condition has become false, because TestandSet has returned a false value. So now Pi escapes the do nothing statement and enters its critical section.

While Pi is in its critical section, suppose there is another process Pj as follows:

```
  do {
      while (TestandSet (&lock))
            ; //do nothing
            Critical Section
  lock = FALSE;              //exit condition
      Remainder Section
  } while (true);
```

Pj is trying to enter its critical section while Pi is executing its critical section. So the value of the lock variable is TRUE (which Pi did) and now Pj calls TestandSet with lock variable true. The TestandSet receives the value true in the target variable. The local variable returnvalue stores that value TRUE. The value of the lock variable is still set to true by *target = TRUE; and the TestandSet instruction returns the value of the returnvalue which is true. So for the process Pj the while condition will be true and it will keep on executing the do nothing statement, so Pj is prevented from entering its critical section.

As soon as process Pi wants to leave its critical section, it will set the value of the lock variable to false and then Pj will again call TestandSet instruction with the value of the variable lock set to false. So it will again call TestandSet with a false value of lock variable and just as Pi got hold of the critical section (while the initial value of lock variable was false) Pj will also get hold of its critical section.

2.5.3 Dekker's Solution

Here the solution uses priority over which thread will enter the critical section. Dekker's solution provides mutual exclusion, freedom from deadlock and freedom from starvation.

```
main()
{
    // tell which thread has highest priority
int turn = 0 ; // or 1 initially
    // flags to indicate if each thread is ready to enter its critical section
boolean wants_to_enter{0] = false;
boolean wants_to_enter[1] = false;
    startthreads();
}
Thread0()
{
    do {
            wants_to_enter[0] = true;
            // wait until thread1 wants to enter its critical section
            while (wants_to_enter[1] == true )
            {
                    // if thread1 has higher priority
                    If (turn != 0)
                    {
                            // give access to other thread
                            wants_to_enter[0] = false
                        //wait until this thread has higher priority
                            while (turn != 0)
```

```
                        ; //do nothing
                    wants_to_enter[0] = true;
                }
        }
        // CRITICAL SECTION
        // give priority to thread1
        turn =1 ;
wants_to_enter[0] = false; // indicate thread0 has completed its critical
section
        //REMAINDER SECTION
  } while (true) ;
    Thread1()
    {
        do {
          wants_to_enter[1] = true;
          // wait until thread 0 wants to enter its critical section
          while (wants_to_enter[0] == true )
          {
            // if thread 0 has higher priority
            If (turn != 1)
            {
              // give access to other thread
              wants_to_enter[1] = false
              //wait until this thread has higher priority
              while (turn != 1)
                        ; //do nothing
              wants_to_enter[1] = true;
          }
    }
      // CRITICAL SECTION
      // give priority to thread 0
      turn =0 ;
```

```
                wants_to_enter[1] = false; // indicate thread1 has
completed its critical section
                //REMAINDER SECTION
    } while (true) ;
```

2.6 Semaphores

With the TestandSet instruction and Peterson's Solution to the critical section problem, it becomes difficult to implement a solution to the critical section problem. Therefore, we use a tool known as semaphore to synchronize the processes. A semaphore is a variable (suppose S) that uses 2 atomic operations wait() and signal(), and it can only be accessed via these 2 atomic operations.

To test whether we can enter the critical section, we use the wait() operation. To leave the critical section, we use the signal() operation.

The code of the wait() operation is as follows:

```
wait( S) {
        while (S <= 0)
                ; //do nothing
        S —;
}
```

The code of the signal operation is as follows:

```
Signal( S) {
        S++;
}
```

The wait() and signal() operations are atomic, i.e. when one is getting modified, the other operation cannot take place simultaneously. Or we can say in other words, when one process is modifying the Semaphore value (S), no other process can modify the same semaphore value at the same time. Also atomic operations means that when the wait() operation is taking place the while loop testing and the decrement takes place together without any interrupt occurring between them.

The semaphore executes in 2 ways:

(1) A Counting Semaphore

(2) A Binary Semaphore

(1) A counting semaphore can take on any number of values.

(2) But a Binary Semaphore takes value of either a 0 or a 1. The solution to the critical section problem is solved by using Binary Semaphores.

The binary semaphores are also called as Mutex locks, since they are locks that provide mutually exclusive nature. If one process is executing on the semaphore value, no other process executes on it.

Suppose there is a semaphore mutex. All the processes which are numbered from P0, P1, P2 .....Pn will share this semaphore mutex which is a binary semaphore. This mutex is initially initialised to 1. 1 indicates that any process can enter its critical section.

The code that every process writes for its critical section is as follows:

```
do {
        wait(mutex);
                //Critical Section
        Signal (mutex);
                //Remainder Section
} while (true);
```

Now initially when mutex is 1, any one process can enter its critical section. When it is entering the critical section, it checks the while condition while (S <= 0) .

Now in this case S is not less than or equal to zero. The mutex variable is received by the S variable in the standard wait() operation. So since while condition is not true (because S =1). It escapes the do nothing part and decrements the value of S or of the mutex. So now mutex becomes 0. (and this process enters its critical section).

The other process which now tries to enter the critical section executes its wait operation. So it checks its while condition. Now since they are sharing the mutex variable, so they are checking while mutex <=0 or S<=0. In this case, the new process will find condition S<=0 TRUE. Since the value of mutex =0. So this process will keep on executing its do nothing statement. And not enter its critical section.

When the first process finishes its critical section, it executes the signal() operation, which will increment the mutex, so mutex will become 1. Now the first process enters its Remainder Section, and the second process which was executing wait(), will now find its while condition to be false. (while S<=0), since mutex =1 now as left by the first process. So while condition will become false and this second process escapes the do nothing and decrements the value of mutex to 0. So that no other process can enter its critical section now.

To Summarise, initially value of mutex = 1, so any process can enter its critical section. When one process is in its critical section, it makes the value of the mutex variable = 0 to indicate that some process is in its critical section, whenever any other process tries to enter its critical section, it finds the value of mutex = 0. So it keeps on waiting in the while loop doing nothing. As soon as that process leaves its critical section, it increments the value of mutex, making it again 1. So now other processes do not find their while condition true, and escape the do nothing and again any one of them will enter its critical section. And will make sure that nobody else enters its critical section by decrementing the value of mutex by S—, making it again =0.

Busy Waiting

When these processes keep checking whether they can enter their critical section or not, they are doing Busy waiting and they are wasting CPU cycles.

So instead of wasting cycles in Busy Waiting, the process blocks itself. To block itself means that the process puts itself in a waiting queue associated with the semaphore and the process state now becomes the waiting state. Now the CPU scheduler selects another process for execution.

The process which is blocked by the semaphore, will need to work when another process executes a signal operation to indicate that it is leaving its critical section. This is done with the help of the wakeup() call, which changes the process state of the waiting process from waiting to ready state.

The process then gets the ready queue, which is the queue ready for execution, skipping all the busy waiting cycles.

To implement the above, we need to change our wait() and signal() code as follows:

```
Typedef node {
    int value;
    node process *list;
} semaphore;
```

Each semaphore has an integer value and a list of processes list.

When a process waits on a semaphore, it is added to the list of processes. The signal process removes one process from list of processes and awakens that process.

The wait semaphore is defined now as follows:

```
wait( semaphore s) {
        S-> value —;
        if (S -> value < 0)
        {
                add this process to S-> list
                block()
        }
    }
```

The signal semaphore code becomes as

```
signal (semaphore s) {
    S-> value ++;
    if (S -> value < = 0 )
    {
        remove a process p from S -> list
        wakeup( p) ;
    }
}
```

The block() operation suspends the process that invokes it. The wakeup (p) operation resumes the execution of a blocked process p. The block() and wakeup (P) are system calls which the operating system provides.

2.7 Process Synchronisation Problems

There are a number of problems which tell how concurrent processes should be synchronized so that they don't enter the critical section at the same time. We will discuss 3 problems here :

(1) Dinning Philosophers Problem

(2) Sleeping Barbers Problem

(3) Readers Writers Problem

2.7.1 Dinning Philosophers Problem

In the Dinning Philosophers problem, there are 5 philosophers who are sitting on 5 chairs. There is a bowl of rice kept in the middle of the table. Each philosopher has a plate to eat and there are 5 chopsticks which are placed between the 2 plates in a round table as follows:

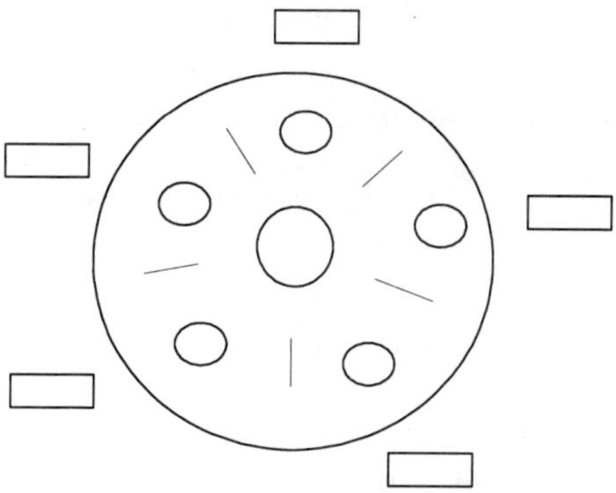

The philosophers are either thinking or they are eating. When they think, they are in the remainder section. When they eat they are in the critical section. The philosophers when eats needs 2 chopsticks which are closest to it, one on his left hand side and the other on his right hand side. He picks them up and starts eating.

A philosopher cannot pick up a chopstick which is already in the hand of another philosopher. When a philosopher has both chopsticks available at the same time, he eats without releasing his chopsticks. When he has finished eating, he will put back both chopsticks back on the table, so that other hungry philosophers can use the chopsticks and eat again.

The dinning philosophers problem is considered a classical synchronisation problem because it is an example of a large class of concurrency control problems.

As you must have understood by now that the chopsticks is the sharable resource between the philosophers. So this sharable resource can be represented by a semaphore to solve the process synchronisation concurrency problem.

Since there are 5 chopsticks, so we need an array of 5 semaphores. To get hold of the chopstick, the philosopher will use the standard wait()

operation and to release the chopstick, the philosopher will use the standard signal() operation. Thus, the shared chopsticks can be represented as follows:

Semaphore chopstick[5];

Where all the elements of chopstick are initialised to 1 (so that any of the 5 philosophers can pick up the chopsticks)

The code of the dinning philosophers problem is as follows:

```
do {
        wait( chopstick[i];
        wait( chopstick[(i+ 1)%5];
        ...
        //eat CRITICAL SECTION
        signal( chopstick[i]);
        signal( chopstick[(i+1)%5]);
        //think REMAINDER SECTION
} while (TRUE);
```

As it is an array, the values the chopsticks takes vary from 0 to 4. Now it is a round table, so the philosopher will pick up one chopstick[i] and it will pick up the next numbered chopstick, so i+1. Now if it picks up the 1st chopstick, then it will pick up the 2nd chopstick. And now if it picks up the 4th chopstick, so now it should pick up the 0th chopstick. So it will be chopstick[4] and chopstick[(4+1)%5] = 5%5 = 0.

Now let us consider what happens when all 5 philosophers are hungry at the same time. So each will grab a chopstick, and no body will be able to grab the second chopstick. So no one will be able to enter its critical section at the same time.

So this is a condition of deadlock, where each philosopher is waiting to get hold of the 2nd chopstick, but none of the 5 philosophers is releasing it. The ways in which we can avoid the deadlock conditions are as follows:

(1) Allow only 4 philosophers to pick up the chopsticks, so that 1 chopstick will be left, and one philosopher will be able to to enter its critical section. When he leaves the critical section (i.e. puts both chopsticks down. The others will be able to enter the critical section.

(2) Allow a philosopher to pick up a chopstick, if both chopsticks, one to his left and one to his right are available or free at the same time. Then he can enter his critical section.

(3) Let an odd philosopher pick up first their left chopstick and then their right chopstick. And let an even philosopher pick up the right hand side chopstick first and then their left hand side chopstick. Let us explain the above with the help of a diagram

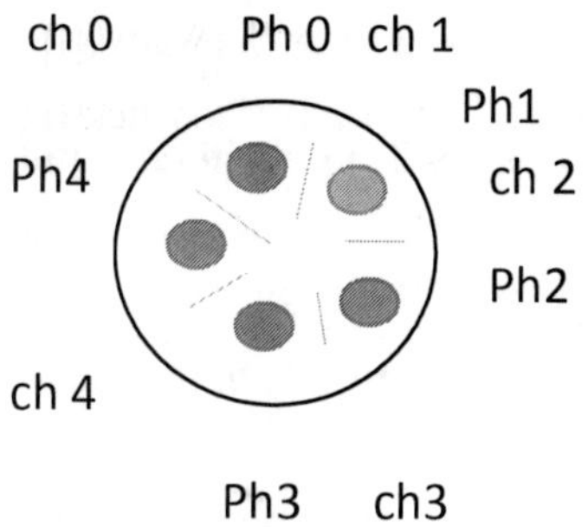

Now the even philosophers are Ph 0, Ph 2 and Ph 4 and the odd philosophers are Ph 1 and Ph 3. So Ph 1 and Ph 3 will pick up their left chopstick first. So left chopstick of Ph1 is ch 2 and left chopstick of Ph 3 is ch 4. Now the even philosophers will pick their right chopstick first. So Ph 0 picks right chopstick which is ch 0, Ph 2 will pick his right chopstick which is ch 2 and Ph 4 will pick his right chopstick which is ch 4. Now Ph 1 and Ph 2 both try to pick chopstick ch 2 first, which is a clash and similarly Ph 3 and Ph 4 try to pick chopstick ch 4 first which is a clash. In this way we can avoid a deadlock.

2.7.2 The Sleeping Barbers Problem

The Sleeping Barber problem is also one of the classical concurrency control problem. A barber shop has n waiting chairs for his customers and one chair for the barber. When the barber is cutting hair, he is in his critical section. When the barber is sleeping he is in his remainder section.

Now if there are no customers, the barber goes to sleep. If one customer comes, he wakes up the barber and the barber starts cutting his hair.

The above diagram shows a barber shop.

If a customer comes and all chairs are occupied, then the customer leaves.

If a customer enters and there are some empty waiting chairs, then he will occupy and sit on the waiting chair empty in the queue.

2.7.3 The Reader's Writers Problem

Some processes only read the database and other processes may write or update the database.

If the processes try to read and write at the same time, then problems will be there.

Whenever a write operation takes place, it has to be done in an exclusive mode which means no other operation takes place at that time.

The Readers Writers problem may be stated in 2 points:

(1) No Reader should wait, unless there is a writer that has taken the permission to access the shared object.

That is, no reader will wait for other readers to finish, simply if a writer is waiting.

(2) Once a writer is ready, that writer performs its write as soon as possible or in other words, if a writer is waiting to access the object, no new reader may start reading.

A solution to either problem may result in starvation. Starvation is the term which is used to indicate that if a process is not given a chance to execute for a long time, because of the fact that other processes keep coming in and that particular process, never gets a chance to execute. So we say that the process is starved.

(1) If the first solution is used, then the writers may starve.

(2) If the second solution is used, then the readers may starve.

Here we give a method to provide the solution of the first Readers Writers problem:

The Reader processes share the following data structures:

```
Semaphore        mutex, writer,
Int              readercount,
```

The semaphores mutex and writer are initialised to 1, and readercount is initialised to 0.

The semaphore writer is accessed by both the reader and the writer processes.

To update the variable readercount, the mutex semaphore is used to ensure mutual exclusion.

The variable readercount keeps track of how many processes are currently reading the object.

The semaphore writer functions as a mutual exclusion semaphore for the writers.

It is also used by the first or the last reader that enters or leaves the critical section.

- It is not used by other readers who enter or exit while other readers are in their critical section.

The code of the writers process is as follows:

```
do {
    wait(writer);
            //writing is performed
    signal(writer);
} while (true);
```

Readers Process:

```
do {
    wait(mutex);
    readercount++;
    if (readercount <= 1)
            wait(writer);
    signal(writer);
            // Reading is performed
    wait(mutex);
    readercount—;
```

```
        if (readercount == 0)
                signal (writer);
        signal(mutex);
} while(true);
```

If one writer is in the critical section and n readers are waiting, then one reader is queued on writer and the rest n-1 readers will be queued on mutex.

When a writer executes signal (writer), we may allow the execution of either the waiting readers or a single waiting writer.

Chapter - 3

Interprocess Communication

3.1 Introduction

Concurrency in operating systems is achieved when more than one process runs in the RAM. Some processes do not disturb the other process's running. Such processes are known as independent processes. They execute simultaneously but at the same time do not affect the other process's running in any way. These processes do not share any data, code segment or files with another process.

When processes affect the running of another process, then they are known as co-operating processes. These processes can share data, code segment and files.

Why do we need co-operating processes? There are a number of factors which are in favour of co-operating processes and they are as follows:

(1) Information Sharing: Many processes may want to affect the same code. An environment should be provided so that they can have access to that code.

(2) Computation Speedup: To achieve a speedup in executing code. We may have a task that can be broken down into subtasks. Each subtask may be executed parallelly and then the results of all the subtasks may be accumulated to give the final result. Here the subtasks have to be executed with a single CPU. So executing processes means that they will be shuffled between CPU and I/O as in the case of multiprogramming systems.

(3) Modularity: There may be times when we want one code to be split up into different modules giving a modular effect.

These co-operating processes would want to exchange information and data amongst themselves. Therefore, they require a mechanism known as Inter Process Communication (IPC) to do so.

3.1 Inter Process Communication

Inter Process Communication may be achieved by any one of the following methods:

(1) Shared Memory

(2) Message Passing

(3) Sockets

(4) Remote Procedure Call (RPC)

(5) Pipes

Please note that out of the methods given above, Sockets, Remote procedure calls and Pipes are implemented using client server communication essentially. Although shared memory and message passing may use client server architecture.

3.1.1 Shared Memory

Shared Memory as the name suggests is done by allocating a region of memory that would be shared among co-operating processes. The processes can read/write from that memory area. Kernel is not involved.

On the other hand message passing is achieved by processes passing message to each other. Kernel is involved.

Message Passing

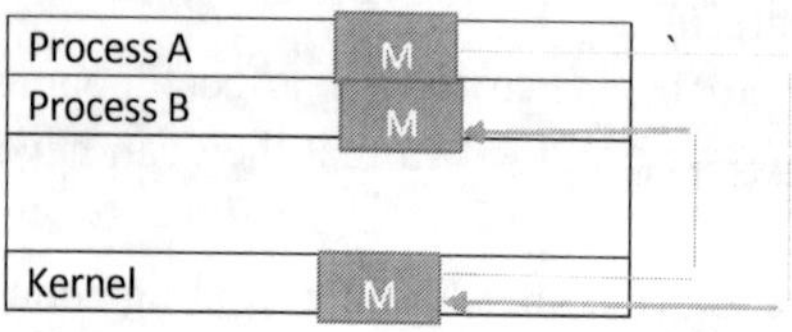

Process A is passing

a message to process B

Shared Memory

Process B writes and Process A reads

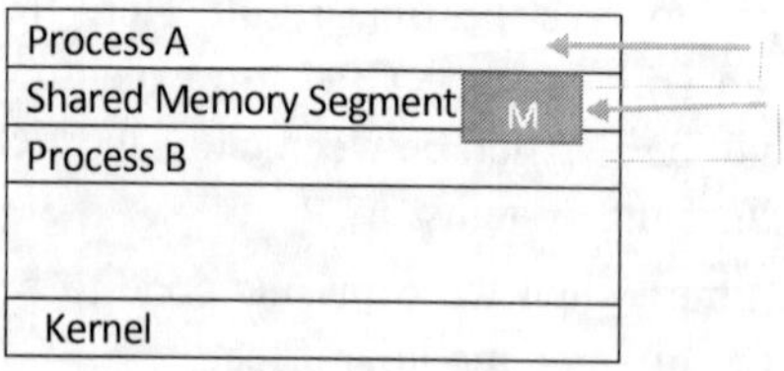

Shared Memory:

(a) Is a convenient way to pass information.

(b) Speed is high.

(c) Is faster than message passing.

(d) To implement shared memory, some assistance is required from the Kernel because of system calls.

(e) Once shared memory is established no more assistance from the Kernel is required. The processes then themselves exchange information.

(f) The system calls are only required to create shared memory region.

(g) The shared memory region is created in the space where processes are lying.

(h) The co-operating processes read/write data into this space.

(i) The processes themselves are responsible for achieving mutual exclusion in the case of write statement. That is no two processes write in the memory area at the same time.

(j) An example of a shared memory concept is the producer consumer problem discussed earlier.

3.1.2 Message Passing System

Message Passing

(a) This system is useful in a distributed computing environment. They do nor rely on sharing the same address space.

(b) In this system, the processes are kept on different computers, which are connected via a network.

(c) An example of this is the whattsapp, where messages are exchanged via world wide web.

(d) The operations used here are send message and receive message.

(e) There can be fixed length messages or variable length messages also.

(f) If two processes, suppose A and B want to communicate. They must send or receive messages from each other.

(g) They need to communicate with each other via a network.

(h) Any one of the following technologies must be employed:

    (i) Direct or Indirect

    (ii) Synchronous or Asynchronous

    (iii) Automatic or Explicit Buffering

3.1.2.1 Direct or Indirect Communication

(A) In Direct communication, each process must explicitly name the sender process or the recipient process.

Two operations are used namely send() and receive()

The send() operation is defined as:

send(P, message) - We send a message to the process named P

the receive() operation is defined as:

receive(Q, message) - We receive a message from process Q.

Further Direct communication is divided into 2 parts:

(a) Symmetry Addressing

(b) Asymmetry Addressing

(a) In direct communication, a link is established between the processes that want to communicate.

It is mandatory for both processes to know each other before communicating.

1. Symmetry Addressing

Both the sender process and receiver process must name each other before communicating.

2. Asymmetry Addressing

Only the sender process needs to name the recipient process explicitly.

The recipient process is not required to name the sender process explicitly.

The send() and receive() processes are defined as follows:

Send(P, message) – we are sending a message to a process named P.

Receive(id, message) – We receive message from any process whose variable is id.

The id variable is set to the process from which we received the message or communicated with it.

B. In **Indirect Communication**

In this system, ports or mailboxes are used for communicating between two processes.

A mailbox is a kind of object from which messages can be removed and in which we can store messages.

In this case, the two processes which want to communicate must share the object mailbox. The operation in this case are defined as follows:

Send(B, message) - we send a message to mailbox B.

Receive (A, message) – we receive a message from mailbox A.

3.1.2.2 Synchronous or Asynchronous Communication

Synchronous means Blocking

Asynchronous means Unblocking

To discuss the above we should be familiar with some terms

(i) Blocking Send – The sending process is blocked until the message is received by the receiving process or the mailbox.

(ii) Non-Blocking Send – The sending process sends the message and resumes operation. There is no condition under which the process is blocked.

(iii) Blocking Receive – The receiver process is blocked until a message is made available.

(iv) Non-Blocking Receive- The receiver resumes in either of the two conditions, A valid Message is received or a null message is there. So no restriction is put on receiving.

Now we can make different combinations of Send() and Receive().

The Producer -Consumer problem is a case where we used blocking send and blocking receive.

The producer performs a blocking send() operation and the consumer performs a blocking receive() operation.

The producer waits until the message is delivered to either the receiver or the mailbox.

Similarly the consumer waits until the message is available.

3.1.2.3 Buffering

Buffering is used for either case, if the communication was direct or indirect. A buffer or a queue is definitely required.

There are 3 types of queues:

(1) Zero Capacity

(2) Bounded Capacity

(3) Unbounded Capacity

(1) Zero-Capacity – The length of the queue is 0. That is no message is kept in waiting state. In this case, the sender is using blocking send, and the receiver receives any message.

(2) Bounded Capacity – There is a finite number, n, of which the capacity of a buffer is. Therefore, at one point of time, n messages can be stored. The new messages can be accepted if the queue is not full. The messages sent by sender are placed in queue, and the sender can continue sending until is full. If the queue is full. Then the sender has to stop sending messages until space is made available by the receiver who can receive one or more messages.

(3) Unbounded Capacity – There is no finite limit of length n in this case. Any number of messages can reside on the queue. Therefore, in this case, the sender never blocks.

Client Server Communication

The following methods must use a client server architecture.

3.1.3 Sockets

To establish a connection between two processes across the network requires the use of sockets. A socket is an endpoint of communication.

In the TCP/IP protocol. An IP address is used to identify a machine on a network. All machines have a unique IP address through which they can be identified on the internet.

The socket contains two fields:

(1) An IP address (to identify a machine)

(2) Port Number (to identify which process on that particular machine)

On a particular machine, different processes are running. The process is identified by the port number on which it is running.

IP = 125.23.4.1 IP = 166.13.1.6.

Port No = 1825 Port No = 80 (http)

In a computer system, there are 2 types of processes that are running.

(1) System Processes

(2) User Defined Processes

The system processes are the ones which specify services already defined, such as ftp, http, telnet etc.

All the well known system processes have port no. 1024 and below.

The processes that are user defined are assigned port numbers from 1025 and above.

A client machine would want to initiate a connection between itself and the server machine. This would be done with the help of a process on a client machine connect to a process on server machine.

A particular process that initiates a request is identified by the IP address of client machine + port number of client machine. The server process which accepts the requests is identified by IP address of server machine + port number of server machine.

These two pairs of end connections are known as sockets.

Considering the example of client and server in the diagram above, we have the pair of sockets as:

The socket of client machine is - (125.23.4.1 : 1825)

The socket of server machine is – (166.13.1.6 : 80)

Now the packets travel from the socket of client to the socket of server.

If another machine wants to connect to the web server. It will have its own socket (different IP address, different port no.) to connect to the socket of web server.

The socket of client machine is - (143.5.4.16 : 1611)

The socket of server machine is – (166.13.1.6 : 80)

If another process on the same machine wants to connect to the web server. It will have its own socket (same IP address, different port no.) to connect to the socket of web server.

The socket of client machine is - (125.23.4.1 : 1622)

The socket of server machine is – (166.13.1.6 : 80)

3.1.4 Remote Procedure Call (RPC)

The RPC functionality can be executed between machines which are connected to the network.

In RPC, the messages are not only packets but a well structured unit called a stub.

A daemon (or a background process) is running on a remote machine at a particular port number. It is just listening, waiting for requests to come.

The message sent by the client machine contains an identifier of the function that has to be executed on the remote machine and the parameters that have to be passed to the function.

After the function is executed on the remote machine, its output is sent back to the requester machine in a separate message.

The requester machine has a port number which is included at the start of the message. A system has one IP address but may have multiple port numbers to distinguish between the many processes of that machine.

When a remote process needs a service, it will address its message to the appropriate port no.

For example, if a machine wants to know who all persons are logged into the system (server). The server would be having a daemon (background process) running this service on a port number say 3022. So all requester systems would send a message to port no. 3022 to obtain the list of current users. The answer would be received in a reply message.

The RPC hides all details required for communication by providing a stub on the client side. For each remote procedure, a different stub is required. When client wishes to execute a remote procedure call (RPC), it calls the appropriate stub and passes in that stub all parameters required for the procedure call.

The stub finds the port number of the process for which the call is intended. The parameters are packaged in such a way that they are ready to be transmitted over the network. The stub then passes the message using message passing.

A similar stub on the server machine receives the stub from client machine and invokes the procedure on the server.

Any return value that needs to be passed to the client machine is done so.

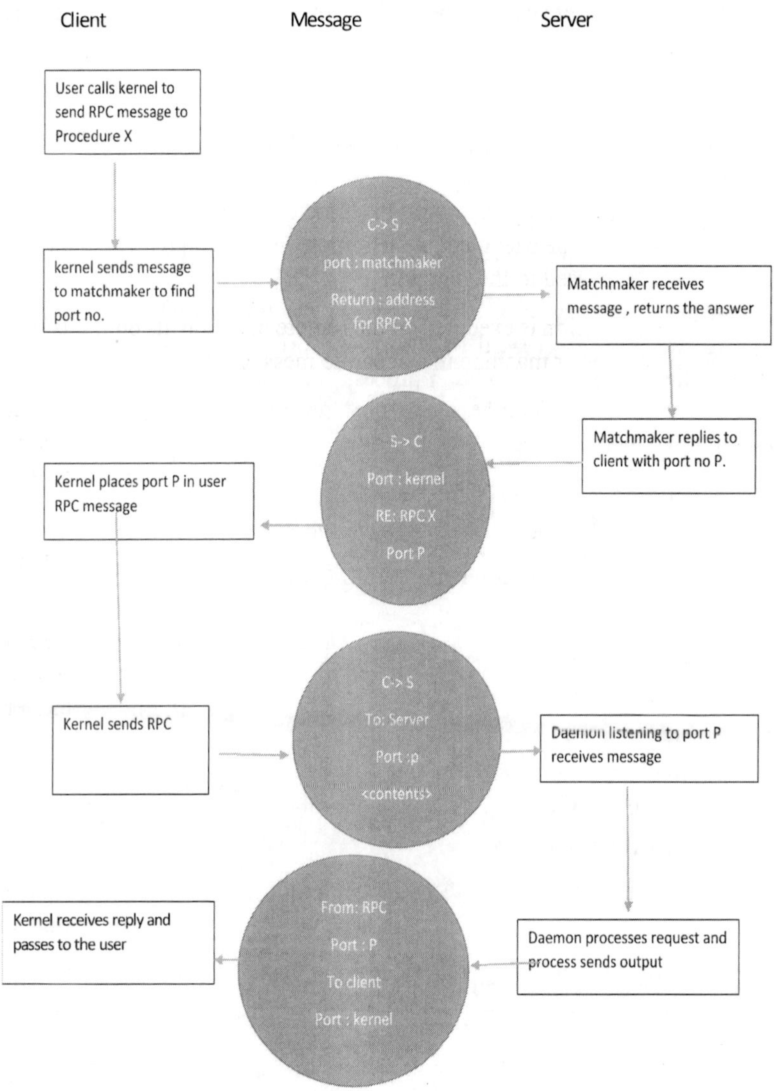

3.1.5 Pipes

Pipes are another way in which inter process communication can be done. Out of the two processes, one is a producer process and another a consumer process. The producer process writes to one end of the pipe (the write end) and the consumer process reads from the other end of the pipe (the read end). Each process can read and write to the pipe.

The pipe() system call can be used to construct a pipe between the two processes in the following manner.

pipe(int fd[])

This function creates a pipe that is accessed through the int fd[] file descriptors.

fd[0] signifies the read end of the pipe

fd[1] signifies the write end of the pipe

A pipe can only be accessed through the process which created it. Typically a pipe is created by the parent process and is used to pass information from parent to child process. The parent process uses fork() system call to create a child process. The fork() system call is explained in detail in the next section.

A child process inherits the files and code from the parent process. Similarly the child inherits the pipe from the parent process.

Take a look at the following program in C language to describe pipes.

```
#include <sys/types.h>
#include <stdio.h>
#include <string.h>
#include <unistd.h>
#defne BUFFER_SIZE 25
#define READ_END 0
#define WRITE_END 1
int main(void)
{
    char WRITE_MSG[BUFFER_SIZE] = "Greetings";
    char READ_MSG[BUFFER_SIZE];
    int fd[2];
    pid_t = pid;
/* create the pipe */
If (pipe(fd) == -1)
{
    fprintf(stderr, "pipe failed");
    return 1;
}
```

```
/* create a child process by fork() system call */
pid = fork();
if pid( < 0)
{
    fprintf(stderr, "fork failed");
    return 1;
}
else if (pid > 0) /* parent process*/
{
    /* close the read end of the pipe which is unused in the parent
                    process */
    close( fd[READ_END]);
    /* write to the pipe */
    write( fd[WRITE_END], WRITE_MSG, (strlen(WRITE_MSG)
                    + 1);
    /* close write end of the pipe after using in parent process*/
    close( fd[WRITE_END]);
}
else { /* child process*/
{
/* close the write end of the pipe which is unused in the child process
    */
close(fd[WRITE_END]);
/* read from the pipe */
read(fd[READ_END], READ_MSG, BUFFER_SIZE);
printf("read %s", READ_MSG);
/*close the read end of the pipe after using in the child process*/
}
return 0;
```

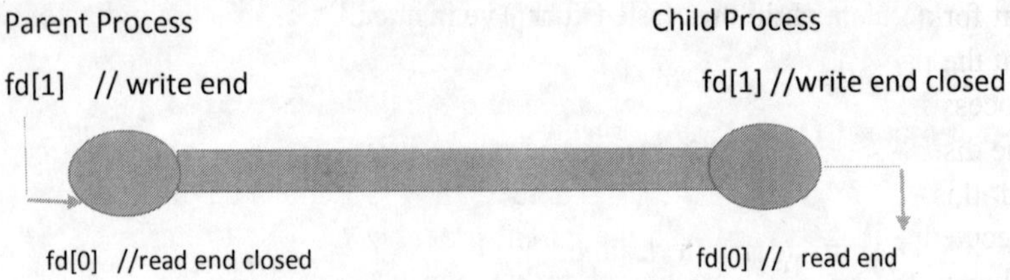

The parent process creates a child process with the help of the fork() system call. The parent has the read end and the write end of the pipe. Similarly the child has the read end and the write end of the pipe. The read end in both processes is denoted as fd[0], and the write end in both the processes is denoted by fd[1].

Now the parent writes to the pipe and the child reads from the pipe. So the parent needs to access its write end for writing and needs to close its read end since it is not going to read anything from the pipe.

Similarly, the child needs to access its read end for reading from the pipe and closes its write end, since the child is not going to write anything in the pipe.

Process Generation

The fork() system call is used for creating a new process. The process created is known as the child process and the process which has created is known as the parent process. The processes are identified according to a unique process identifier (pid) which is typically an integer number.

When a parent process creates a new process, there are two ways in which the execution takes place.

(1) The parent continues to execute concurrently with the child process
Or

(2) The parent waits for the child process to complete first and then the parent would execute itself.

In Unix, each process is identified by its process identifier, which is a unique integer.

The new process is created by the fork() system call. The parent and the child continue to execute the instructions with one difference. The return value of fork() system call is either 0, +ve integer or a -ve integer. The -ve integer indicates that the fork() system call was not executed properly and that fork() system call has failed. The +ve integer in the process indicates that the parent process is executing and the 0 means that the code of child process is executing. Both the parent and the child have duplicate code. The distinguishing factor is that, in parent process, the if statement having pid>0 is executed and in the child process the if statement having pid=0 is executed. This is because to the parent process, the fork() returns a +ve value and to the child process the fork() returns a 0 value.

Take a look at the program below in C language to demonstrate the use of fork() system call. We use a wait() system call in the parent process to say that the parent waits for the child to finish executing first and then the parent executes. The child process is using the execlp() system call to execute the "ls" command in "/bin" directory of the Unix operating system.

```
#include <sys/types.h>
#include <stdio.h>
#include <unistd.h>
int main()
{
    pid_t pid;
    /* fork a child process */
    pid = fork();
    if (pid < 0) /* -ve number indicates that error occurred */
            {
            fprintf(stderr, "fork failed");
            return 1; /* unsuccessful completion */
            }
    else if (pid == 0) /* 0 indicates a child process */
            {
            execlp("/bin/ls", "ls", null);
            }
else /* +ve value indicates parent process */
{
    /* parent waits for child to complete */
    wait(NULL);
    print("child complete");
}
```

```
return 0; /* successful completion of the program */
}
```

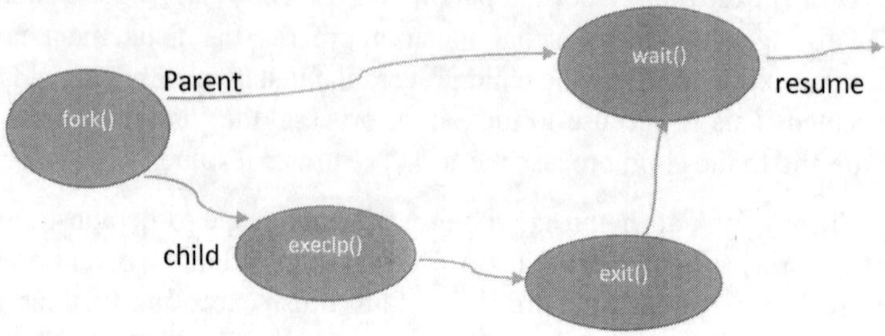

Chapter - 4

The Central Processing Unit

4.1 Introduction

In a memory system, when many processes reside, we try to keep the CPU busy for maximum time so that the throughput can be greater.

In a multi programming environment, the program is either doing an I/O cycle, which in other words is called an I/O burst cycle. And at other times, the program is doing a CPU cycle (ALU unit is working), so that is called a CPU burst cycle.

When a program spends more time in executing CPU burst cycles than I/O burst cycles, then it is called a CPU bound program.

When a program spends more time in executing I/O burst cycles then CPU burst cycles, then it is called an I/O bound program.

An I/O Bound Program looks like this:

I/O Burst	CPU Burst	I/O Burst	CPU Burst	I/O Burst

A CPU Bound Program Looks like this:

CPU Burst	I/O Burst	CPU Burst	I/O Burst

4.2 CPU Schedulers

The processes which need CPU time are all present in the ready queue. Whenever the CPU is sitting idle, it needs to be given some process from the ready queue, so that it starts executing the process and is no longer in the idle state. This is the work of the short term scheduler. The short term scheduler would select a process from the list of processes in memory that are ready to execute and then allocate any 1 process to the CPU. The CPU will execute it and then the short term scheduler will select another process from the ready queue and give CPU that process to execute. So this way the scheduler keeps the CPU busy all the time. The ready queue may be a FIFO or a Priority Queue.

4.2.1 Pre-Emptive Scheduling

Pre-emptive by the name suggests that you can stop the process from running in between and do not wait for its completion to take place whereas non pre-emptive scheduling means you cannot stop the process in between while it is running, but wait for its completion.

There are 4 cases in which a process may change its state.

(1) A process may go from a running state to a waiting state under the following circumstances.

  (i) An I/O request takes place or

  (ii) When a parent process goes to a waiting state, so that its child process completes its execution

(2) A process may change state from running state to ready state. This may take place when an interrupt occurs.

(3) A process may change state from waiting state to ready state. This takes place on completion of an I/O event.

(4) When a process terminates.

Non pre-emptive scheduling means, when we cannot have any control over the scheduling of processes. They cannot be stopped, once started they have to complete and only then they stop.

So in cases 1 and 4, when a process changes state from a running state to a waiting state or when a process terminates, we have no control over it. They have to take place, they cannot be interrupted in between.

In the 2 and 3 case, i.e. when they change from a running state to a ready state or when they change from waiting state to a ready state. Then they can be interrupted in between. The CPU can be handed over to another process and the process can be stopped in between.

As said earlier, that when an interrupt takes place or on completion of an I/O event, a signal can be sent to stop the CPU from working on a process and hand over the CPU to another process.

4.2.2 Dispatcher

The dispatcher is responsible for giving the control of the CPU to the process that has been selected by the short term scheduler.

The functionalities that the dispatcher has to perform are as follows:

(i) Switching Context

Context switching means that the process which is running, all of its variables, states and other information has to be saved in its process control block, so that when it restarts, it can start from where it had left.

(ii) Switching to user mode

This means that the user mode takes control. So that the switching of processes is easier.

(iii) Jumping to the proper location

When the control is handed over to the new process, then jumping to the proper location in the new program so that, that program can start executing.

4.3 Scheduling Criteria

There are a number of CPU scheduling algorithms, which decide in which order the processes have to be selected for processing.

Different algorithms can be used in different situations. Before we discuss the different CPU scheduling algorithms, there are many criteria on the basis of which CPU algorithms can be compared.

These are as follows:

1. CPU Utilisation: The CPU should be busy as much as possible. The utilisation of a CPU can range from 0 to 100 %. But in real case scenarios, it generally varies from 40 to 90%.
2. Throughput: It is the number of processes that are completed per unit time. For very long processes, this state may be one process per hour. For short processes, it can go upto ten processes per second.
3. Turnaround Time: Turnaround Time means how much time does a take to complete. This is the time taken from the time of submission of a process to the time of completion of a process.

   The total turnaround time is taken for doing all of the following activities or the summation of the time spent in doing the following activities:

   (i) The time spent in getting into the memory

   (ii) The time spent in waiting into the ready queue.

(iii) The time spent in executing on the CPU

(iv) The time spent in doing I/O activities.

4. Waiting Time: Waiting time as the name suggests is the time that the process spends in waiting in the ready queue. It does not take into account the time spent in doing CPU activity or the time spent in doing the I/O activity.

5. Response Time: The response time as the name suggests is the time taken it takes to give the first response. It is basically the time taken from the time of submission of a request (or a process) to the time taken to give the first response.

4.4 CPU Scheduling Algorithms

Multi programmed systems came into existence because we could perform scheduling of processes between I/O and CPU. We can utilise the computer system in an optimal way by switching among CPU processes.

A process executes till the time that it needs to wait to perform some I/O request. If the computer system is simple, the CPU would be put to wait until the I/O gets completed.

This waiting time leads to wasting of the CPU time and no useful work is performed in that time.

The alteration between the CPU and I/O takes place as follows: When CPU cycles are executed by one process, the I/O can be given to another process. And when the 1st process finished CPU, if it wants I/O, then I/O is granted. Meanwhile if any other process is waiting for CPU, the CPU can be granted.

A process's execution can be defined as consisting of CPU cycles and I/O cycles. In a program, if the code is performing some Arithmetic or logical operation, it is said to be running CPU cycles. And when in that process some read or write operation takes place, it is said to be executing I/O cycles.

The process's execution alternates between I/O cycles known as I/O burst and CPU cycles known as CPU burst.

The CPU burst in a program may vary to a great extent.

Normally there are a large number of small CPU bursts and a small number of long CPU bursts.

In concurrent programming, we have a number of processes running and waiting to acquire the CPU. To achieve multiprogramming, we allocate the CPU to different processes as per their need. The processes reside in ready queue waiting to get the CPU. The scheduling algorithms tells how the process will acquire the CPU and in which order.

There are a number of scheduling algorithms which we will discuss:

(1) First Come First Serve (FCFS)

(2) Shortest Job First (SJF)

(3) Shortest Remaining Time First (SRTF)

(4) Priority Scheduling

(5) Round Robin Scheduling

4.4.1 First Come First Serve (FCFS)

First Come First Serve as the name specifies, is that a process which came first to ask for the CPU, will be granted the CPU first. There is a First In First Out (FIFO) queue, which is known as the ready queue. The process which needs the CPU will attach its process control block (PCB) to the tail of the queue. When the CPU is free, it will pick up the process from the head of the queue. The process is then removed from the head of the queue, so that next process in line becomes the head of the queue.

Disadvantage: There is a slight disadvantage with this scheduling algorithm. The average waiting time of the processes is often too long.

Let us take an example to show. Let there be processes and their burst time as follows:

Process	Burst Time
P1	20
P2	4
P3	4

If the arrival of processes is in the order of P1, P2 and then P3 and they are served on FCFS basis, then the Gantt Chart will be made as follows:

P1	P2	P3	
0	20	24	28

A Gantt Chart is a bar chart which shows, at what time the process started execution, at what time did it finish execution and in what order did the processes execute.

The above diagram says that the process P1 started at time 0 and finished its execution in 20 ms. After that process P2 started at time 20 and finished its execution at time 24. Then P3 started at time 24 and finished its execution at time 28.

So the waiting time is calculated as

0 for process P1

20 for process P2

24 for Process P3

So the average waiting time is as follows:

(0 + 20 + 24) / 3 = 44/3 = 14.66 ms

Now if the processes arrive in the order say P2, P3 and then P1.

So the Gantt Chart will be as follows:

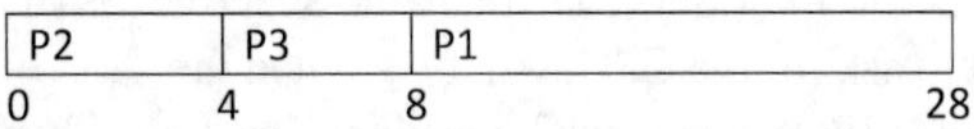

The waiting time for

P2 is 0

P3 is 4

P1 is 8

So the average waiting time is as follows:

(0 + 4 + 8) / 3 = 12/3 = 4 ms

We can see that the waiting time has reduced substantially. So it infers that the waiting time is constrained with the order of arrival of processes.

FCFS is a Non-Preemptive algorithm, which mean that when one process starts executing with CPU. The other process cannot come and grab the CPU from the already running process. When the running process finishes its execution, only then CPU is granted to another process.

This is the problem that Non-Preemptive algorithms face. Each process would get a share of CPU at regular intervals cannot be guaranteed. To have one process running all the time can lead to disastrous consequences.

Before we explain the next algorithm, let us have a quick look at the turnaround time of FCFS algorithm.

The turnaround time for a process is, the time process finished execution minus the time it was submitted into the system.

So taking the above example, whose Gantt Chart is as follows:

P1	P2	P3
0	20	24	28

The time that processes P1, P2 and P3 are submitted is 0, since their arrival time is not indicated. But order is P1, P2 and then P3.

Process	Burst Time	Arrival Time	Completion Time
P1	20	0	20
P2	4	0	24
P3	4	0	28

Turn around time =

P1 is 20 – 0 = 20

P2 is 24 – 0 = 24

P3 is 28 – 0 = 28

Average Turnaround Time is (20 + 24 + 28) / 3 = 24 ms

4.4.2 Shortest Job First (SJF)

A Process's CPU Burst decides which process will execute next. When the ready queue is empty and then a process arrives, it is started because it is the only one that can be executed. Meanwhile the first process is executing, a number of processes arrive. The CPU after finishing the first process will now take up the process which has the smallest burst time. If there are two processes having the same burst time. Then they will be taken by the CPU on FCFS basis to break the tie between them.

Let us take an Example to explain this.

Process	Burst Time
P1	8
P2	9
P3	7
P4	4

Since no arrival time is given, so we take arrival time as 0 for all the processes. And we assume that they are all available in the ready queue from which the CPU has to take processes.

The Gantt Chart will look as follows:

P4	P3	P1	P2

0 4 11 19 28

The waiting time for each process is as follows:

P4 is 0

P3 is 4

P1 is 11

P2 is 19

So average waiting time = (0 + 4 + 11 + 19) /4 = 8.5 ms

Now solving the above example with FCFS algorithm would be

P1	P2	P3	P4

0 8 17 24 28

The waiting time with FCFS is

P1 is 0

P2 is 8

P3 is 17

P4 is 24

So the average waiting time = (0 + 8 + 17 + 24) / 4 = 12.25 ms

Which shows that other algorithms perform better than FCFS.

Let us calculate the Turnaround time for this example (SJF)

Process	Burst Time	Completion Time
P1	8	19
P2	9	28
P3	7	11
P4	4	4

P1 is 19 – 0 = 19

P2 is 28 – 0 = 28

P3 is 11 – 0 = 11

P4 is 4 – 0 = 4

Average Turnaround time = (19+28+11+4) /4 = 15.5 ms

4.4.3 Shortest Remaining Time First (SRTF)

The disadvantage that SJF has is that we need to know the length of the next process. Picking a lower length process may lead to faster response. SJF is good for long term scheduling. Long term scheduling means that processes are selected from secondary memory. For short term scheduling, SJF is not good. Short term scheduling means picking processes from the ready queue. In the case of short term scheduling, we cannot determine the length of the next CPU burst.

So we have to introduce pre-emption. SJF can be either pre-emptive or non-preemptive. Pre-emptive means we can stop a process's execution while the process is running. Non-Preemptive means once a program starts executing, it cannot be stopped in between.

The example of SJF given above is a type of non-preemptive scheduling. When SJF works with pre-emption, then we say it can be stopped in between if a new process with smaller length arrives. This gives rise to Shortest Remaining Time First (SRTF) scheduling.

When the next CPU burst of the newly admitted process is shorter than that is left of the currently executing process. Then we stop the currently executing process and start executing the process which has the smaller length. Note that the checking is done at every time unit. If there is anyone shorter of the current process. The current process is stopped.

To explain this, let us take an example. Consider the following scenario

Process	Arrival Time	Burst Time
P1	0	7
P2	1	3
P3	2	8
P4	3	4

The processes arrive at the ready queue at the time shown along with their burst time.

The resulting pre-emptive SJF will give the following Gantt Chart:

P1	P2	P4	P1	P3	
0	1	4	8	14	22

Process P1 started at time 0. Since it is the only process in the queue, therefore it starts executing. At time 1, process P2 arrives, the remaining time left for process P1 is 6 ms. The time for process P2 is 3 ms which is shorter than that of P1. So process P1 is preempted and process P2 starts executing. At time 2, process P3 arrives, but it is bigger (8 ms) than P2 (2 ms). So P2 continues. At time 3, process P4 arrives, but it is bigger (4 ms) that the current process P2(1 ms). At time 4, process P2 finishes, and then the other processes are executed as per the criteria.

The waiting time (Time it started executing minus the time it arrived) is calculated as follows:

P1 : 8 – 1 - 0 = 7 (8 for time it started, 1 for already done 1 unit, 0 for arrival time)

P2 : 1 – 1 = 0 (1 for it started, 1 for arrival time)

P3 : 14 – 2 = 12 (14 for it started, 2 for arrival)

P4 : 4 – 3 = 1 (4 for it started, 3 for arrival)

Average Waiting Time = (7 + 0 + 12 + 1) /4

= 20/4 = 5 ms

The Turnaround Time (Time it Completed minus the time it was submitted) is as follows:

P1: 14 – 0 = 14 (14 for completed, 0 for submitted)

P2 : 4 – 1 = 3 (4 for completed, 1 for submitted)

P3: 22 – 2 = 20 (22 for completed, 2 for submitted)

P4: 8 – 3 = 5 (8 for completed, 3 for submitted)

Average Turnaround Time = (14 + 3 + 20 + 5) / 4

= 42/4 = 10.5 ms

Let us compare the pre-emptive SJF to non pre-emptive SJF.

For non- pre emptive SJF, the Gantt Chart will be as follows:

P1	P2	P4	P3	
0	7	10	14	22

P1 started executing at time 0. Since that was the only process present in the ready queue at time 0, so it started executing. As P2 came at time 1, P1 did not stop because we cannot stop any process in between. Once started, they have to finish only then the other process can be given a chance.

The Waiting Time is as follows :

P1: 0 – 0 = 0

P2: 7 – 1 = 6

P3 : 14 – 2 = 12

P4 : 10 – 3 = 7

Average Waiting Time = (0 + 6 + 12 + 7) / 4

= 25/4 = 6.25 ms

We can see that the waiting time of SRTF (5 ms) is less than that of SJF (6.25 ms)

Let us calculate the Turnaround Time as follows:

P1: 7 – 0 = 7

P2: 10 – 1= 9

P3: 22 – 2 = 20

P4: 14 – 3 = 11

Average Wating Time = (7 + 9 + 20 + 11) /4

= 47/4

= 11.75 ms

Average Turnaround Time in SRTF (10.5 ms) is less than that of SJF(11.75 ms).

4.4.4 Priority Scheduling

Every process has a priority associated with it. The highest priority process gets the chance to execute on CPU. If the priority for 2 processes is same, then FCFS will be applied. The priority is indicated by a numeric value of fixed range such as 0 to 7 or 0 to 400. Some systems use number 1 to represent the highest priority. Other systems may use number 1 to indicate lowest priority.

In the following example, we use number 1 to represent highest priority. Consider the following processes to arrive at time 0 with the priority given in the order P1, P2, P3, P4, P5.

Process	Burst Time	Priority
P1	8	3
P2	3	1
P3	2	4
P4	2	5
P5	6	2

Using Priority scheduling, we would schedule these processes according to the following Gantt Chart.

P2	P5	P1	P3	P4

0 3 9 17 19 21

The waiting time is

P1 = 9 – 0 = 9

P2 = 0 – 0 = 0

P3= 17 – 0 = 17

P4 = 19 – 0 = 19

P5 = 3 – 0 = 3

Average Waiting Time = (9 + 0 + 17 + 19 + 3) / 5

= 48/5

= 9.6 ms

The turnaround time is as follows:

P1 = 17 – 0 =17

P2 = 3 – 0 = 3

P3 = 19 – 0 = 19

P4 = 21 – 0 = 21

P5 = 9 – 0 = 9

Average Turnaround Time = (17 + 3 + 19 + 21 + 9) / 5

= 69/5

= 13.8 ms

Priority Scheduling can be pre-emptive and non pre-emptive also. A pre-emptive priority scheduling algorithm will stop executing its lower priority process, if a higher priority process arrives in between.

In the case of a non pre-emptive priority. The process will simply be put at the head of the queue. The example considered above is a case of non- pre-emptive priority scheduling.

Let us take an example of a pre-emptive priority scheduling. Suppose the following processes arrive at a given times with given priorities.

Process	Arrival Time	Burst Time	Priority
P1	0	6	3
P2	1	3	1
P3	2	5	2
P4	3	4	4
P5	4	8	5

So the Gantt Chart is as follows:

P1	P2	P3	P1	P4	P5
0	1	4	9	14	18	26

The waiting time is as follows:

P1 = 9 – 1 – 0 = 8

P2 = 1 – 1 = 0

P3 = 4 – 2 = 2

P4 = 14 – 3 = 11

P5 = 18 – 4 = 14

The Average Waiting Time = (8 + 0 + 2 + 11 + 14) / 5

= 35/ 5

= 7 ms

The Turnaround Time

P1 = 14 – 0 = 14

P2 = 4 – 1 = 3

P3 = 9 -2 = 7

P4 = 18 – 3 = 15

P5 = 26 – 4 = 22

The Average Turnaround Time = (14 + 3 + 7 + 15 + 22) / 5

= 61/5

= 12.2 ms

Priority Scheduling can lead to starvation. Starvation occurs when one process is sitting to be executed by the CPU, but higher priority processes keep coming before it gets a chance to execute and CPU is continuously allotted to higher priority processes. The problem of starvation can be solved by a method by a method known as ‘Aging’. In aging we increase the priority of a process which has waited long enough. Example, if priorities of a process range from 125 (low) to 0 (high). Then we may increase the priority of a process by subtracting 1 after 20 minutes. So eventually a process will get priority 0 and will get executed since it has the highest priority.

4.4.5 Round Robin Scheduling (RR)

When processes need to share the CPU, in case of multitasking systems. We need to give time to each process. So that all processes get executed without anyone of them be starved.

In Round Robin scheduling, there is a time quantum also known as time slice given to each process which represents the time in milliseconds given to each process for executing. This is implemented like a circular queue. The job which comes is attached to the end of the circular queue. The time slice is generally 10 ms upto 100 ms.

The CPU goes in circular way giving time slice to each process. The first process is picked, it is executed for the given time quantum. Then it stops executing after the time slice gets over. Now the CPU picks the 2nd process in the circular queue, gives it the time slice, and when time slice is over. The next process gets it. When a process is assigned the time slice, two conditions may occur:

(1) The process requires time units less than the time slice allotted. In which case the process will voluntarily give up when its execution finishes and time slice will be given to next process.

(2) The process requires time unit greater than the time slice allotted. In this case it will execute for the whole time slice and then give up when time slice is over. Next time round when the CPU will come in circular fashion, it will give the time slice again. And the process will start from it had left not repeating what it had done before.

Round Robin is executed by allotting a timer to each process at the end. When timer is over, the operating system sends an interrupt to the executing process, asking it to stop. The process does a context switch. Context switch means that all the values of variables, registers and files is saved, so that when the process resumes execution in the next cycle, it will start from where it had left and not repeating the work already done.

Consider the following :

Time Slice 4ms and arrival time is 0 for all.

Process	Burst Time
P1	16
P2	8
P3	3

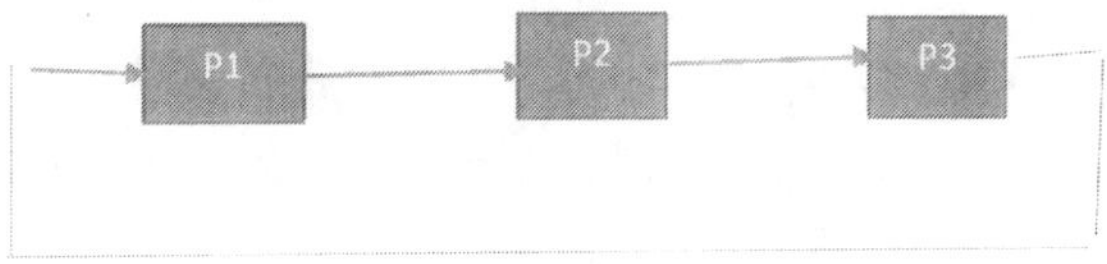

The process P1 gets the first time slice of 4 ms. Since it requires 16 ms to complete, it completes 4 ms and then hands over the time slice to the process P2. P2 requires 8 ms, so it also executes for 4 ms and then hands over the time slice to P3. Process P3 requires only 3 ms to complete. So it will execute for 3 ms and not 4 ms. Since its execution time is less than the time slice, so it will not waste any time, and after 3 ms, it will voluntarily give up. So the Gantt Chart is as follows:

P1	P2	P3	P1	P2	P1	P1	
0	4	8	11	15	19	23	27

The waiting time is calculated as follows:

P1 : 19 – 8 – 0 = 11

P2: 4 – 0 = 4

P3 : 8 – 0 = 8

Average waiting time = (11 + 4 + 8)/ 3

= 23/3

= 7.67 ms

The Turnaround Time is

P1: 27 – 0 = 27

P2: 19 – 0 = 19

P3: 11 – 0 = 11

The Average Turnaround Time = (27 + 19 + 11)/3

= 57 / 3

= 19 ms

The Round Robin technique can also be implemented with different arrival times. Consider the following with time slice of 4ms.

Process	Burst Time	Arrival Time
P1	22	0
P2	3	5
P3	7	2

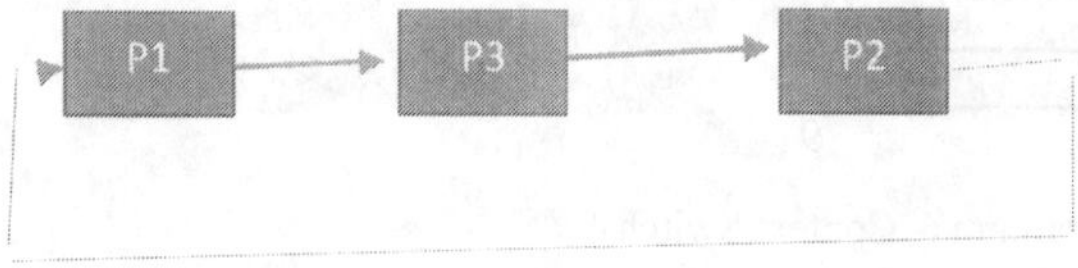

The Gantt Chart is as follows:

P1	P3	P2	P1	P3	P1	P1	P1	P1	
0	4	8	11	15	18	22	26	30	32

The Waiting Time is calculated as

P1: 18 – 8 – 0 = 10 (18 for waiting that long, 8 for work already done, 0 for arrival time)

P2: 8 – 5 = 3 (8 for waiting, 5 for arrival time)

P3: 15 – 4 – 2 = 9 (15 for waiting that long, 4 for work already done, 2 for arrival time)

Average Waiting Time = (10 + 3 + 9) / 3
= 22/3
= 7.33 ms

The Turnaround Time

P1: 32 – 0 = 32 (32 for time it completed, 0 for arrival time)

P2: 11 – 5 = 6 (11 for time it completed, 5 for arrival time)

P3: 18 – 2 = 16 (18 for time it completed, 2 for arrival time)

Average Turnaround Time = (32 + 6 + 16) / 3
= 54/3
= 18 ms

The performance of a Round Robin scheduling depends on the size of a time slice. In case the time quantum of very large size, it starts behaving like FCFS. Suppose we have a time slice of 12 ms and our process is only for 9 ms. Then the process will need only 1 time slice. If the time slice is 6 ms, then our process will require only 2 time slices. So in this the process does not spend too much of time doing context switching. If the time slice is 1 ms, then with round robin 8 context switches will be required. So the CPU will waste most of its time in doing Context Switching other than doing some useful work.

Time Quantum 12, Context Switch 0

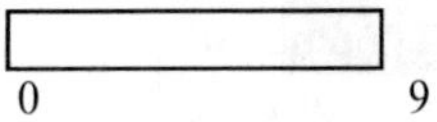

Time Quantum 6, Context Switch 1

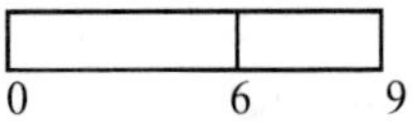

Time Quantum 1, Context Switch 8

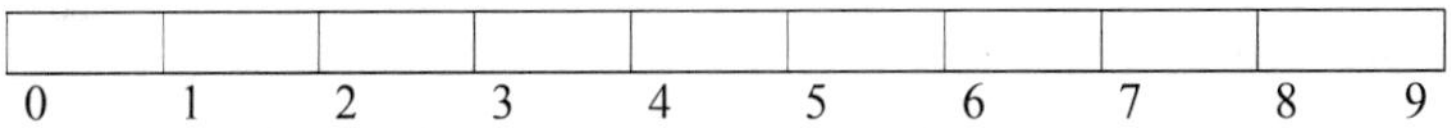

4.5 Multiprocessing

We should not have CPU busy most of the time doing Context Switching, because that wastes a lot of CPU time. Ideally 80% of the time CPU should spend on working. When the number of CPUs are more than 1, then the scheduling problem becomes more complex. With Multiple CPUs, we require load sharing. There are two ways in which CPUs can work together.

(1) Asymmetric Multiprocessing

(2) Symmetric Multiprocessing

In asymmetric approach, we have 1 master CPU, which controls the other CPUs which are slave to it.

The master CPU is responsible for taking decisions, I/O processing and other system related activities. The slave or other CPUs only execute the user code. In symmetric multiprocessing (SMP) there is no master slave relation. All CPUs have equal responsibility. Here the processes do self scheduling. The processes maybe lined up in a common ready queue or else each processor would maintain its private queue. Each processor examines the ready queue and selects process for execution.

4.5.1 Processor Affinity

Processor Affinity as the name suggests is that a processor starts liking a process for execution and wants that process to keep executing for that processor. The reason is that when a process starts executing with a processor, it populates the cache memory for frequently used instructions. Successive accesses to the RAM are done by accessing the cache only and RAM is no longer required. Now if the process migrates to another processor, the contents in the cache are no longer of any use. We would need to invalidate those contents in the cache and populate the cache with new contents of another process which has come to execute with the processor.

Most SMPs processors want that their initially assigned processes should work with them because the cost of invalidating the cache and repopulating it is too much.

4.5.2 Non Uniform Memory Access

In an ideal situation, the CPU and memory are placed on a single board for faster access. If the processor needs to access the memory from another board, then it will slow down the process. So it tries to avoid accessing the memory from another board.

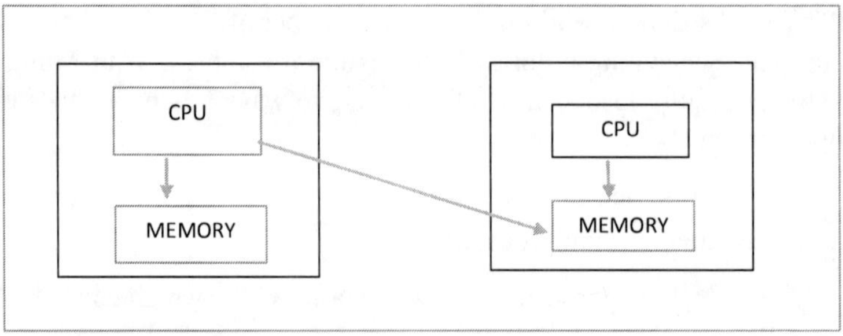

4.5.3 Load Balancing

Load Balancing is a task used for processors who use the SMP architecture and it is important for all CPUs to be equally occupied. To get the multiple CPUs fully utilised, we need to make sure that all processor's workloads are equally balanced. When the processors share a common queue, load balancing is taken care of automatically. But when each processor has its own private queue, we need to access the queue which is larger, and extract processes from it and attach those processes to a smaller/ empty queue of another processor.

There are two types of techniques which are used in load balancing:

(1) Push Migration

(2) Pull Migration

Push Migration

In Push Migration, there is a task which is continuously monitoring the queues of each processor. When ever it finds an imbalance, it will assign the processes to a less busy processor by moving or pushing the processes of the busy processor's to the idle processor's.

Pull Migration

In Pull Migration, there is no such activity that checks the status of queues. But whenever a processor gets idle. It will take the processes from a busy processor's queue and attach to its own self's queue.

The pull and push migration should be carried out in mutually exclusive fashion. Both of them cannot be executed at the same time. But in application scenarios, they work in parallel to one another.

4.5.4 Multicore Processors

Multicore Processors is a term coined when a number of processors which are put together on a single chip. You must have heard of the terms dual core and quad core. In Dual Core, 2 processors are fixed on a single chip and in Quad Core, 4 processors are put on a single chip. Each processor has its own set of register sets for execution and thus appears as a single entity to the user.

Multicore Processors complicate scheduling of CPU. When a processor needs some data from the memory, it may have to wait long enough for the data to become available.

When a processor is waiting for data to become available, it is described as memory stall. This occurs due to a number of reasons such as a cache miss (accessing a data that is not in the cache). It may be possible that a processor spends 50% of its time waiting for data to become available from memory. To take care of the above situation, the hardware allows multiple threads to be assigned to each core. If a thread is waiting for a memory stall (memory to become available), then the core can switch to another thread.

A normal cycle of CPU and Memory stall is as follows:

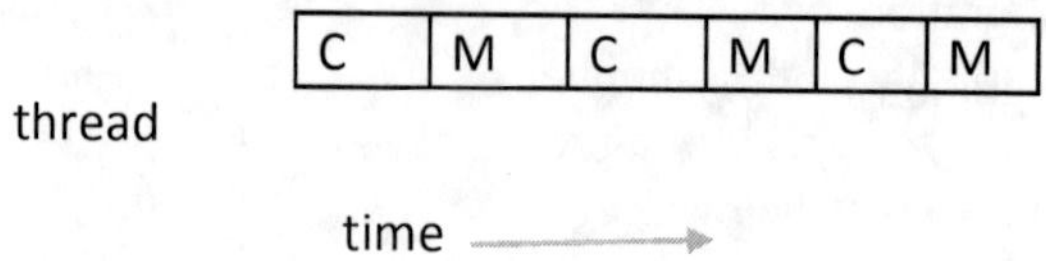

C stands for Compute Cycle
M stands for Memory Cycle

Here is an example of 2 threads running on a single core in an interleaved fashion.

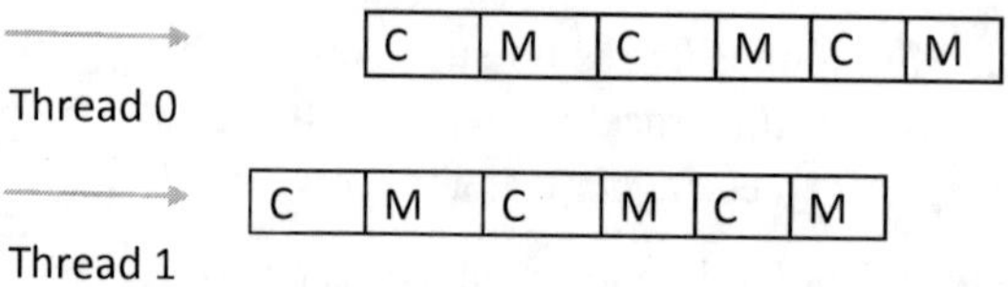

On a given time frame, the thread 1 uses CPU when thread 0 is using memory and thread 1 is using memory when thread 0 is using CPU.

The multithreading occurs on a processor in 2 ways:

(a) Coarse Grained Multithreading

(b) Fine Grained Multithreading

The above is an example of coarse grained multithreading when 1 thread executes on a processor till an event such as a memory stall occurs. We know that the memory stall takes a lot of time, that is why the processor switches to another thread to execute it.

The cost of switching between threads is generally very high, because we need to empty the instructions from the instruction pipeline before the other thread can begin execution on the processor.

Once the instruction pipeline is empty, the new thread starts execution by filling its own instructions in the pipeline.

The fine grained method of interleaving switches between threads at a much finer granuality level. In which we have the fetch-decode-execute instruction cycles. Here the threads are interleaved at the boundary of the instruction cycles. The cost of switching between threads in this case is small.

4.6 Process States

A process goes through a number of states while completing its execution. The current activity of a process defines its state. The various number of states are given below:

(1) New: The process began its execution.
(2) Running: The CPU is executing instructions of the process.
(3) Waiting: The process is waiting for some event to take place such as I/O completion or reception of a signal.
(4) Ready: The process lies in the ready queue, waiting for the CPU to be assigned to it.
(5) Terminated: The process has completed its execution.

Please note that here we are talking about a single processor, who is shuffling between different processes. And only one process can be allotted the CPU at a particular instance of time. There may be a number of processes which are ready to be executed and waiting in the ready queue. But the processor will execute only one process at a time.

The state diagram is as follows:

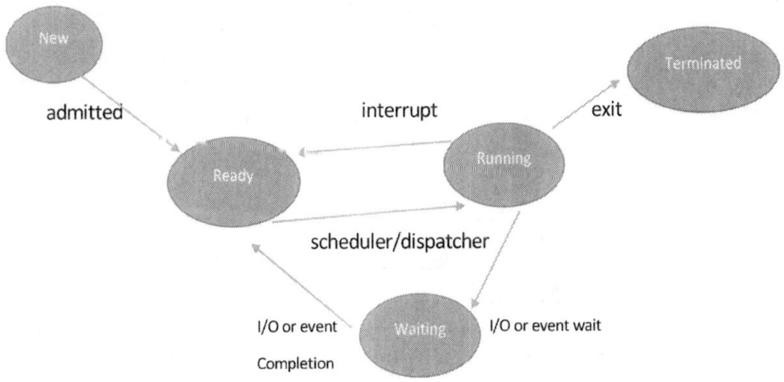

The above diagram indicates that when a process enters, its state is new and it is admitted into the system and is attached to the ready queue.

The short term scheduler assigns a process the CPU and it starts executing, which means going to the running state. While running, an interrupt may occur which is of higher priority than the running process. So in that case, the process is but back to ready queue and the process for which interrupt had occurred starts executing. While running, the process may require to execute some I/O. So it is assigned to waiting state, until the I/O is complete. Once the I/O is complete, the process is put back in the ready queue.

4.7 Process Control Block

Each process is identified by a process control block (PCB) in an operating system. It contains all the specifications associated with a process.

The structure of a PCB is shown below:

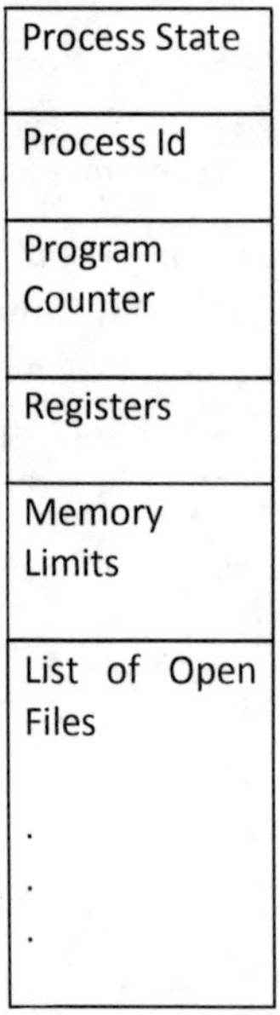

(1) A Process State indicates the state in which a process is currently in. E.g., ready, running, waiting, etc.

(2) Program Counter represents the address of the next instruction which has to be fetched by the CPU for execution.

(3) CPU Registers are the ones which this process is using. The registers are different in number, depending on the computer architecture.

The basic registers are as follows:

(1) Accumulator

(2) Index Register

(3) Stack Pointer

(4) General Purpose Register

The values in all these registers are saved when an interrupt occurs, so that after the interrupt, these registers can continue working from where they left and need not go back to the initial state.

(4) CPU Scheduling Information: This contains all the information that would be needed while the CPU is scheduling processes. Mainly includes the priority of a process, if priority scheduling algorithm is used.

(5) Memory Management Information: This includes all the information that is related to memory. The values of base register and limit registers are included. The page table and segment tables are also stored.

(6) Accounting Information: All the information related to operating system usage is stored. Such as the amount of time spent in doing CPU cycles. The time limits.

(7) I/O Status Information: All information related to I/O that a process has. Such as the list of files open and all the I/O devices which the process is currently using.

PCB stores all the information related to a process and obviously it varies from one process to another.

4.8 Scheduling Queues

To exploit the CPU running at all times, we use a concept of multiprogramming to maximize CPU utilisation.

Time Sharing is another technique used to switch between processes frequently so that all processes have interaction with the user. To achieve this the scheduler has to select one process among many waiting processes.

In case of a single processor, there will only be a single process running at a time, and the rest of the processes have to wait for their turn to come.

As the processes enter the system, they are attached to the job queue. Ready queue stores all the processes which reside in the primary memory (RAM) and are waiting to be executed by the CPU. Ready queue is normally stored as a linked list. The ready queue has pointers pointing to the head and tail of the queue, which is the first and the last PCBs in the list respectively. Each PCB includes a pointer to point to the next PCB in the ready queue.

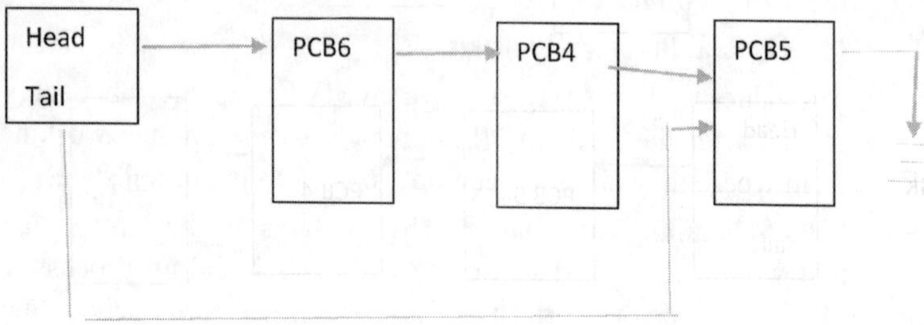

The process which is executing by the CPU ultimately is stopped when one of the following condition takes place.

(1) An Interrupt Occurs

(2) The process requests for some I/O

Now if the process makes an I/O request to a disk drive. As we know that there are a number of processes in the system and the disk may be busy catering the I/O request of some other process. So all the processes desiring the disk drive have to wait in the queue for disk.

Each device has its own queue in which the processes can wait to access that particular device.

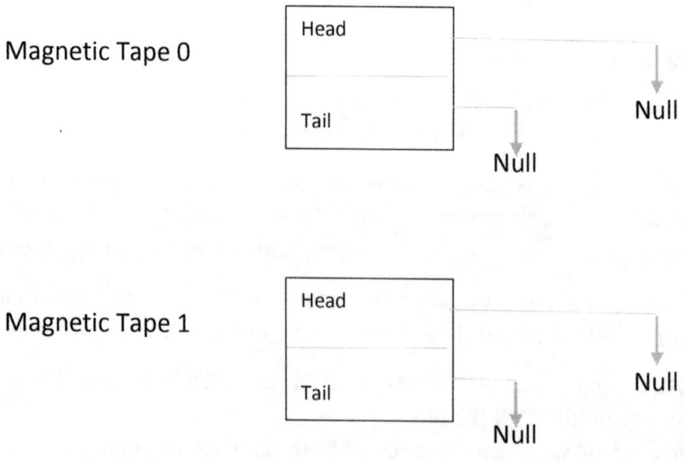

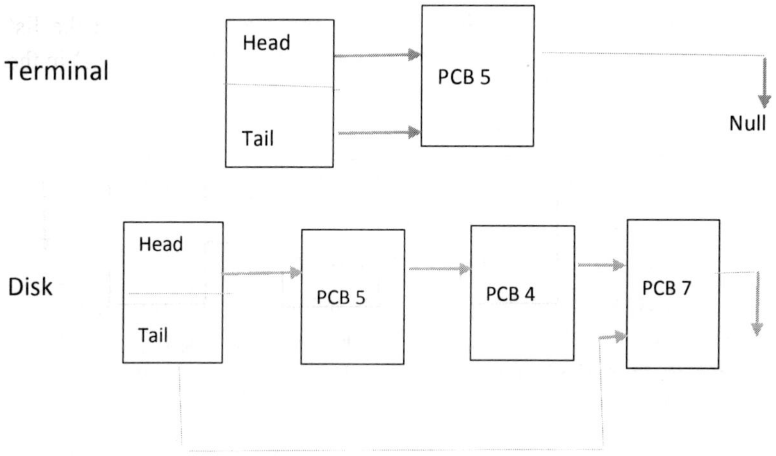

Process scheduling is best represented by queuing diagram given below.

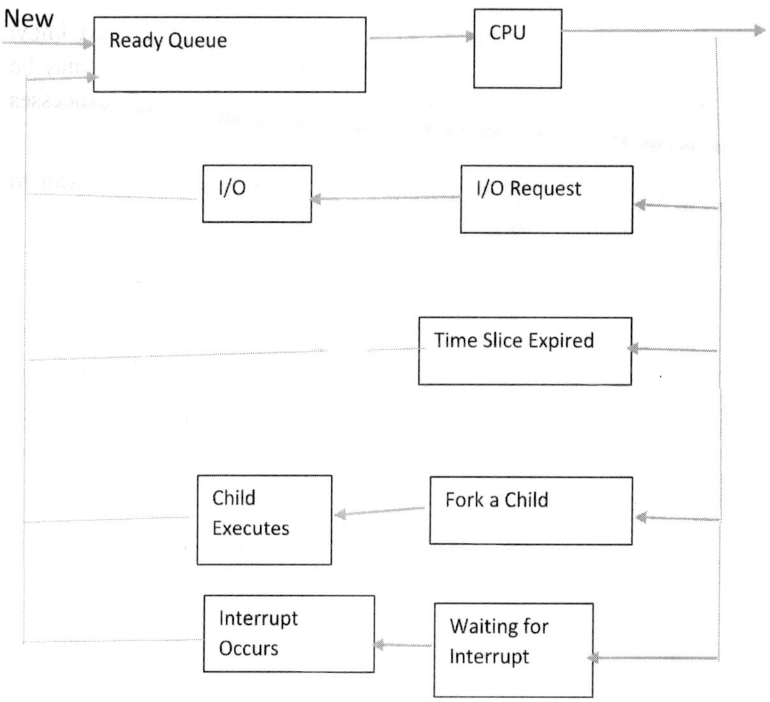

A new process first enters into the ready queue, it sits in the ready queue until it is selected for execution or is dispatched. The process once executing can be stopped because any one of the following reasons:

(1) The process needs to do I/O and therefore is placed in the I/O queue and removed from the ready queue.

(2) The process creates a new child process and therefore is waiting for the child process to get over.

(3) The process is removed forcibly from the CPU, because an interrupt occurred and therefore is put back in ready queue.

(4) If the scheduling used is Round Robin technique, then the process is stopped when its time slice gets over and put in the ready queue for the next cycle of the time slice to be issued to it.

In the cases (1) and (2) of the above, the process gets to the waiting state and once the waiting state is over, it switches back to the ready state and is put back in the ready queue.

The process continues to rotate in this cycle until the time that it gets over. Once it is over, it is terminated and its process control block (PCB) is removed from all the queues and all its resources get deallocated.

4.8.1 Multilevel Queue Scheduling

Processes are classified into 2 types:

(1) Foreground Processes

(2) Background Processes

The foreground processes are interactive with the user. One process's response time needs may differ that from the other process. Even for scheduling, they may have different requirements.

Foreground processes may have priority over background processes. Multilevel queue scheduling has the responsibility of partitioning the ready queue into a number of separate queues.

According to the property of the process, the processes are permanently assigned to one queue. The property of the process may be

(1) Memory Size

(2) Process Priority

(3) Process Type

The different queues may have different scheduling algorithms running on them. For example, separate queues might be used for foreground and background processes. The foreground queue might be using a Round Robin algorithm and the background queue may be using FCFS algorithm. In addition the queues themselves may be scheduled in say implementing a fixed priority pre-emptive scheduling.

Generally foreground queue has absolute priority over the background queue. The queues in order of priority may be depicted as follows:

(1) System Processes (Highest Priority)

(2) Interactive Processes (Foreground)

(3) Interactive editing processes

(4) Batch Processing (Background Processes)

(5) Student Programs (Lowest Priority)

The queue at number 1 has absolute priority over the queues at position 2 to 5. Similarly each numbered queue has higher priority over the queues numbered below it.

The process in the Batch Queue cannot be executed until all the system processes, interactive processes and interactive editing processes are all empty.

As it is a fixed priority pre-emptive scheduling. So if an interactive editing process enters the system and a batch processing process is running. The batch processing process will be pre-empted and chance will be given to higher priority interactive editing process.

4.8.2 Multilevel Feedback Queue Scheduling

In Multilevel Queue, processes are fixed in the queue and cannot be changed. Here processes are free to move between the queues. The basis of putting processes in separate queues is because of the CPU burst. If a process has to take a lot of CPU time, it is put on a lower priority queue. The processes which are I/O bound or interactive are put in a higher priority queue.

Consider the following scenario:

Queue 0

Queue 1

Queue 2

Scheduler first executes all processes of queue 0. When queue 0 is empty, only then it will execute processes in queue 1, and processes in queue 2 will be executed only if queue 0 and queue 1 are empty.

A process that arrives in queue 1 will pre-empt the process of queue 2. Similarly process in queue 0 will pre-empt the processes in queue 1.

Whenever a process enters the ready queue, it is put in queue 0. Suppose a process in queue 0 has been allotted the time slice of 8 ms. If it fails to finish within this time, it is shifted to the tail of queue 1. When queue 0 is empty, the process at the head of queue 1 is given a time slice of 16 ms. If it does not finish in this time slice, it is pre-empted and put into the queue 2. The processes of queue 2 will only execute when queue 0 and queue 1 are empty. This executes in FCFS basis.

If a process is having CPU burst time 8 ms or less, it is given priority. Such processes will be allocated CPU quickly, they will finish the CPU burst and goes off to next I/O burst processes that need more than 8 ms but less than 24 ms. Long processes are automatically given queue 2 and they serve in FCFS order.

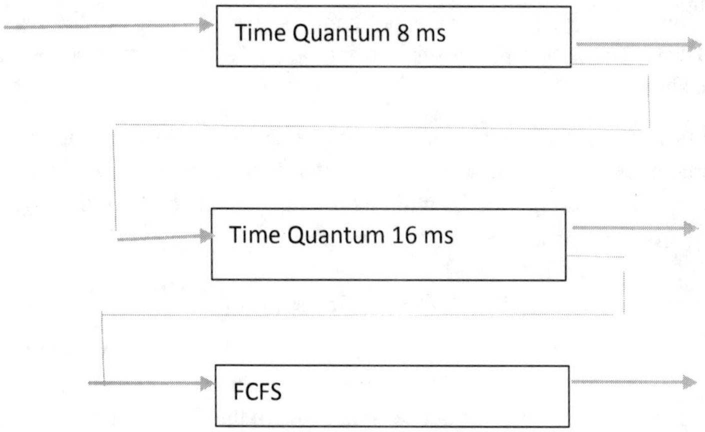

4.9 Schedulers

A process keeps shuffling between various scheduling queues throughout its life cycle. The operating system is responsible for fetching these processes from the queues in a particular fashion. The scheduler selects the process which has to be executed next. In a Batch OS, the number of processes submitted is more than the number of processes executed immediately.

The processes are kept on a mass storage device such as a disk. They stay there until the scheduler selects it for execution. The process of storing processes in a mass storage device is known as spooling.

Long Term Scheduler and Short Term Scheduler

The long term scheduler also known as job scheduler has the responsibility of fetching the processes from the pool and loading them into the RAM for execution.

The short term scheduler also known as CPU scheduler selects the processes from the ready queue to execute, and then CPU is allocated to the selected process.

Both the schedulers work at different frequencies. The short term scheduler needs to select new processes for the CPU pretty frequently. The process executes for only a few milliseconds before waiting for an I/O request.

The short term scheduler executes at least once every 100 ms.

The short term scheduler must act quickly, since the time between execution is short.

The long term scheduler has less frequency of occurrence compared to the short term scheduler.

Long term scheduler can take many minutes between selecting a new process.

Long term scheduler is responsible for the degree of multiprogramming. The degree of multiprogramming refers to the number of processes lying in the RAM at the same time for execution.

The job of long term scheduler is to see that the degree of multi-programming is stable. That is the rate of processes entering the RAM and the rate of processes leaving the RAM must be constant.

When a process leaves the queues, then the long term scheduler should act to bring in another process from the spool.

The long term scheduler can afford to take time to select which process to bring into the RAM, since there is longer interval of time between the execution of 2 processes.

A process is either CPU bound or I/O bound. The I/O bound process spends more of its time executing I/O cycles than the CPU cycles.

A CPU bound process spends more of its time executing CPU cycles than I/O cycles.

The long term scheduler should pick up a mix of CPU bound and I/O bound processes. In case if there are more number of I/O bound processes then the ready queue will almost always be empty. The short term scheduler will be sitting idle.

In case if there are more number of CPU bound processes, then the device queues will almost be empty most of the time. The devices will be less utilised and short term scheduler will be busy. This will cause imbalance in the system.

Medium Term Scheduler

Medium term scheduler has the responsibility of keeping the degree of Multiprogramming constant. Sometimes it becomes necessary to remove.

Adding the medium term scheduler to the queuing diagram:

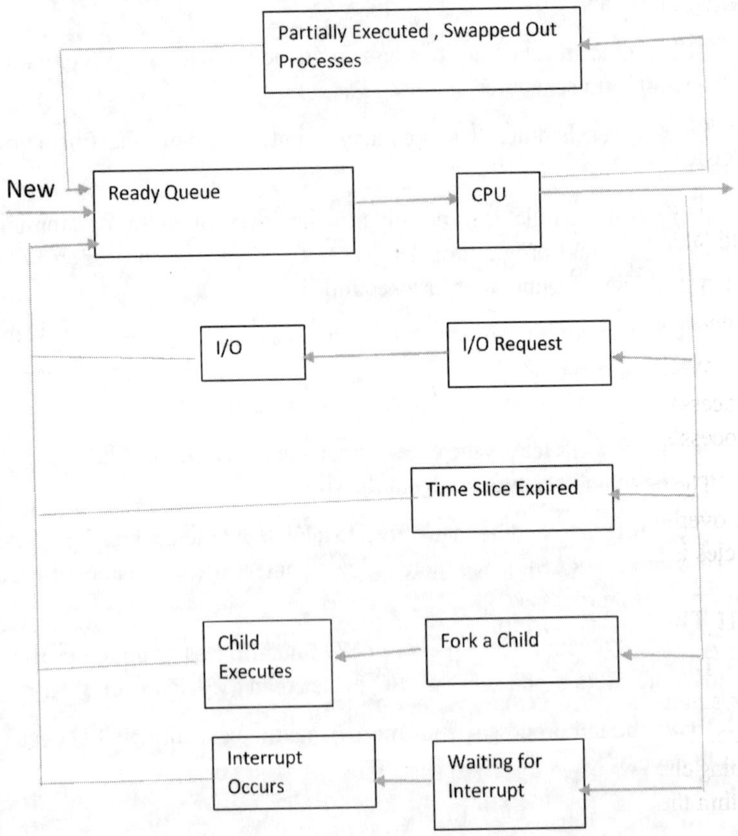

processes from the Ready Queue. So that there are less number of processes requiring the CPU. These removed processes can later be added to the Ready Queue, they can continue execution from where they left.

This is known as swapping. The processes are swapped out of the Ready Queue and later swapped in by the medium term scheduler. When the memory is full due to its overcommitment, it needs to be freed up. The available memory can then be utilised by the remaining processes therefore enhancing efficiency.

4.10 Context Switching

When an interrupt occurs, the CPU is forced to leave its current task and run a kernel routine. This operation is frequently seen.

To cater the interrupts, the system needs to first save all the contents of the current task of the CPU. So that when the task is again given the chance to execute, it will start from the place where it stopped and need not do any re-work.

The process in other words is suspended and later resumed. All the content is available in the PCB of the process. It includes the value of CPU registers, the process's state and all the memory management information.

The state-save is performed which stores the current state of the CPU, and later a state-restore is performed to resume operations.

This switching of the CPU from one to another process performing state-save and state-restore is known as context switching.

When a context switch occurs, the kernel saves the contents of old process's on that process's PCB and loads the saved contents of the new process's (which has just been allotted the CPU) into the RAM.

The time that Operating System takes to do context switching is purely an overhead. Because in this no useful work such as CPU cycle or I/O cycles is taking place, in other words no useful work is carried out.

4.11 Threads

Till now we have discussed a process and that process is called a thread for single process execution. This single thread performs one task at a time. The user is not able to execute 2 processes simultaneously such as typing characters in say a word document and also running the spell checker within the same process.

Multithreading is a concept used in a process which has multiple threads running in one process. So more than one task can be performed at a time.

The process control block is expanded to store the information of all threads running under that process.

The thread is composed of:

(1) Thread Id
(2) Program Counter
(3) Register Set
(4) Stack

The threads within the same process share:

(1) Code Section
(2) Data Section
(3) Open Files
(4) Signals

A heavy weight process or a traditional process has a single thread of control. If a process has multiple threads of control, then these threads can perform multiple tasks at the same time.

The following figure shows how single thread processes look.

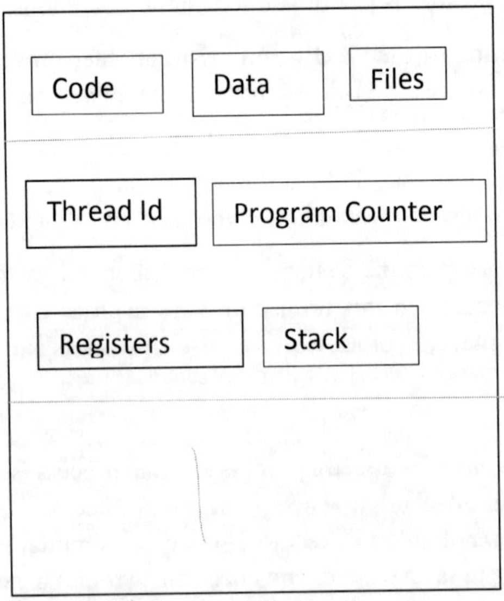

In today's world many s/w packages facilitate multithreading. Example, a web browser may have a thread for displaying images, another thread for retrieving data from network. A word processor may have 1 thread for displaying graphics, another thread for spell checking in the background, yet another thread for interacting with the user through keyboard strokes.

In client server system, these are performed more effectively. A number of clients at the same time might request to a single server. The server then processes these requests and sends back the output to the client programs.

If the above scenario is implemented with a single thread, then the thread of the server would take the request from the first client and process it. The requests coming from other clients will have to wait till the time the thread has finished executing the first client's request. So other client requests may have to wait long enough.

The solution to the above is to have one process listening at the server side. It will receive requests from various clients. Create a new process each for each of the client request. The newly created process will service the client request. The server can then be left with a background process listening at its port. Creation of a process takes a lot of time. To avoid this overhead, one process creates multiple threads. The multithreaded process looks as follows:

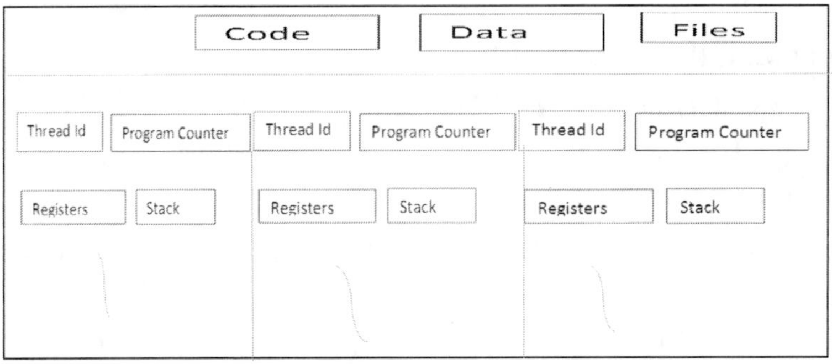

So as it can be seen in the multithreaded system, the code, data and files can be shared among multiple threads. The multiple threads each has its own program counter, Thread Id, Register set and stack.

Multithreading in RPC Servers

When a server receives a request, it creates another thread to execute the request. In this manner the server can cater many requests at the same time. Most Operating System kernels are multithreaded, which means operate in the kernel. Each thread has been given a specific task to perform, such as managing a device and handling an interrupt.

Advantages of Threads

(1) Responsiveness : The program responds to a user even if some part of it is blocked or is performing a lengthy task. For example, a web browser will interact with the user in 1 thread and another thread of the same process is suppose downloading an image.

(2) Sharing of Resources: Resources can be shared by either message passing or shared memory. These have to be explicitly arranged by the programmer. The threads share memory and resources by default. This allows multiple threads running in the same address space.

(3) Economy: Since the memory and resources are shared, the threads take less time to be created. Also context switching takes less time. The process's creation and management takes more time than that of a thread.

(4) Scalability: The threads are able to run parallelly in a multi-processor architecture. A single threaded process has to run on a single processor even if more than one processor exists. Multiple threads run on a multi CPU machine supporting parallelism.

4.12 Multithreading Models

Multithreading occurs at 2 levels:

(1) User Level

(2) Kernel Level

At user level, user threads execute and at kernel level, kernel threads execute.

User level threads do not require the support of a kernel, whereas kernel level threads do require the support of an operating system.

A relationship between the user thread and kernel thread is mandatorily required.

The relationship can occur in one of the following ways:

(1) Many to One Model

(2) One to One Model

(3) Many to Many Model

Many to One Model

In this model, many user level threads are mapped to one kernel level thread.

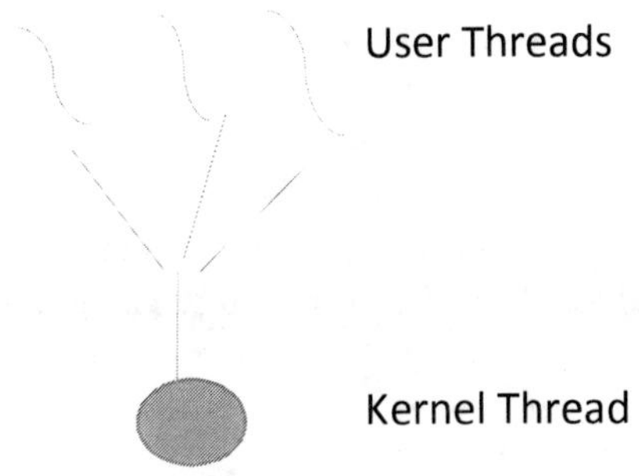

As there is only one kernel level thread, it has to manage all the user level threads. So in this case concurrency cannot take place. Multiple threads cannot run at the same time in multiprocessor systems.

One to One Model

Each user thread is mapped to each kernel thread. So many processes can execute simultaneously. Since there are more than one kernel thread, so concurrency can take place.

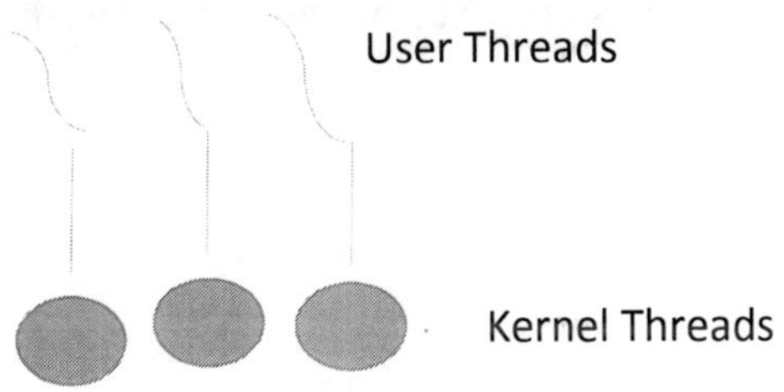

The problem with this is that for each user thread to execute, we require a separate kernel thread. The performance in this case becomes a consideration, since the overhead of creating separate kernel threads degrades the performance.

Many to Many Model

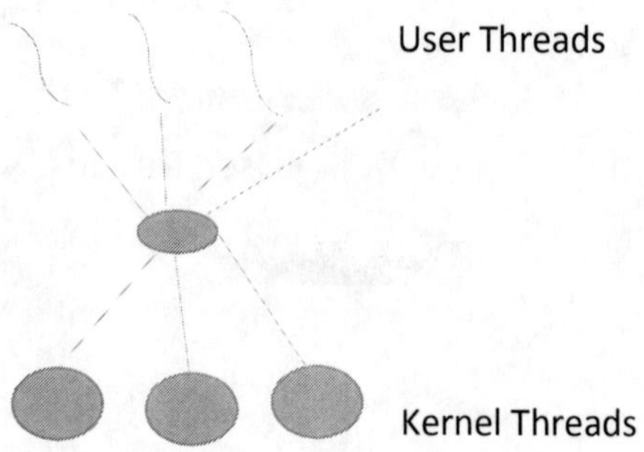

Here the threads work in a multiplex way. Larger number of many user threads are mapped to smaller number of kernel threads.

A particular machine or a particular application may have their kernel level threads allotted to them. A multiprocessor machine may have more kernel level thread allotted to it than a uniprocessor machine.

Many to One Model has to deal with the drawbacks of concurrency. One to One Model has the drawback of creating a large number of kernel threads. The Many to Many Model does not suffer from any of these shortcomings. Since here the users may have any number of threads being created. And accordingly the corresponding kernel threads can run in parallel on a multiprocessor machine. Also if one kernel thread is executing and it performs a blocking system call, then another kernel thread can take over to process it.

Chapter - 5

Deadlocks

5.1 Introduction

When finite number of resources are present, then in a multi-programming environment many processes may want to access these resources.

A process may request for a resource and if that resource is busy catering to another process, then the resource will not be granted to the requesting process. And the requesting process will go in the waiting state until the resource is released. Once released it can be granted to the requesting process.

A process may go on waiting in the same state, because the resource that has been requested by it, is never given to it because the resource may be held by another waiting process.

Such a situation is described as a Deadlock.

5.2 Necessary Conditions for a Deadlock

If the following 4 conditions are true at the same time, then we say that a deadlock is existing.

(1) Mutual Exclusion

(2) Hold and Wait

(3) No Pre-emption

(4) Circular Wait

(1) Mutual Exclusion: A resource can be held by only one process at a time. Suppose there is a process P1 which is currently holding a resource and there is a process P2 that wants access to this resource. The process P2 has to wait until the process P1 releases it.

(2) Hold and Wait: A process say P1 is already holding a resource and that process P1 wants another resource which is held by say process P2, then process P1 is waiting for process P2 to release the resource.

(3) No Pre-emption: The resource held by a process cannot be disrupted in the middle forcefully. The process which holds it should release them on its own after the process finishes its task.

(4) Circular Wait: The waiting of processes forms a loop. Consider a set of processes{P0, P1 P2}, P0 wants a resource held by P1, P1 wants a resource held by P2, P2 wants a resource held by P0.

5.3 Resource Allocation Graph

Resource Allocation Graph is a directed graph which is commonly used for describing deadlocks. The graph consists of set of vertices V and a set of edges E.

There are 2 types of vertices in a resource allocation graph.

(1) Vertices for Processes

P = {P1, P2 ....Pn}

(2) Vertices for Resources

R = {R1, R2 ...Rm}

P is a set consisting of all active processes running in the system.

R is a set of all resource types available in the system.

An edge Pi -> Rj is used to describe that process Pi is requesting for an instance of the resource type Rj and that the process Pi is waiting for an instance of resource Rj to be allocated to it.

An edge Rj -> Pi means that an instance of a Resource type Rj is granted to the process Pi. This means that the allocation of the resource type Rj has been done to Pi.

The request edge is denoted as Pi -> Rj where Pi has requested Rj

The assignment edge is denoted as Rj -> Pi where Rj is assigned to Pi

The process vertex is denoted by a circle

The resource vertex is denoted by a rectangle.

The resource type Rj consists of many instances (A resource may be a printer, and the number of printers available are the instances of the resource type printer). The resource type Rj is a rectangle and the instances of the resource type are depicted by dots in the rectangle.

A request edge points to the rectangle, from the circle. And an assignment edge points to the circle from one of the dots of the rectangle. When a request comes from a process, it is simply pointed to the rectangle of the resource type. When an assignment of a resource has to be done to a process. It specifically tells which instance of the resource type has to be assigned to the process. So the edge comes from dot of a rectangle to the circle of the process.

When the request is fulfilled, then the request edge automatically becomes an assignment edge. When the process is done with all the resources, it releases the resource and the assignment edge is automatically deleted.

Example of Resource Allocation Graph

Consider 3 sets

P = {P1, P2, P3}

R = {R1, R2, R3, R4}

E = {P1 -> R1

P2 -> R3

R1 -> P2

R2 -> P2

R2 -> P1

R3 -> P3}

The instances of the resource types are as follows:

R1 = 1 instance

R2 = 2 instances

R3 = 1 instance

R4 = 3 instances

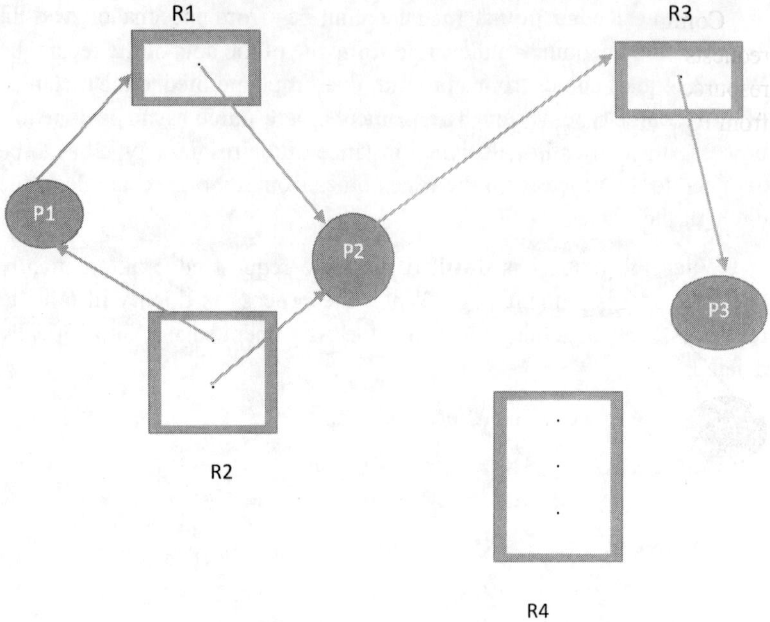

The states of processes are as follows:

P1 is holding an instance of R2

P1 is waiting for an instance of R1

P2 is holding an instance of R2

P2 is holding an instance of R1

P2 is waiting for an instance of R3

P3 is holding an instance of R3

The processes, resources and their corresponding edges are shown in the resource allocation graph above.

If a resource allocation graph does not contain a cycle, then it is said that processes are not deadlocked. And if a graph does form a cycle, then it is said that the processes are deadlocked.

The cycle would exist if the processes are holding single instance of a resource. And if the resources are having more than 1 instances, a cycle exists between 1 instance, then it is said that the processes are not deadlocked, because more instances of resources are free and they can be given to requesting processes.

Coming back to the resource allocation graph, suppose that process P2 requests for an instance of resource type R2. Since all the instances of resource R2 are busy and there is no free instance, then a request edge from P3 -> R2 is added to the graph.

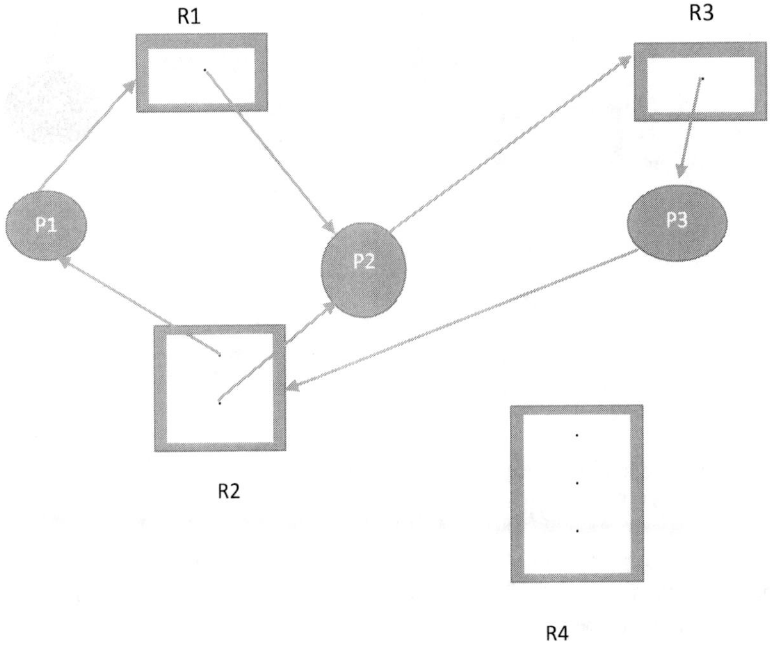

Suppose we consider the Resource Allocation Graph as above.

Over here we see that the graph is having 2 cycles.

(1) P1 -> R1-> P2-> R3->P3 –> R2 -> P1

(2) P2 -> R3-> P3-> R2 -> P2

Therefore, we say that the processes P1, P2 and P3 are deadlocked.

Here P2 is waiting for a resource R3, which is a single instance of it and is held by P3. Process P3 is waiting for an instance of R2. R2 has 2 instances which are held by process P1 and P2. Also P1 is waiting for R1, which is held by P2.

Suppose we have the following Resource Allocation Graph:

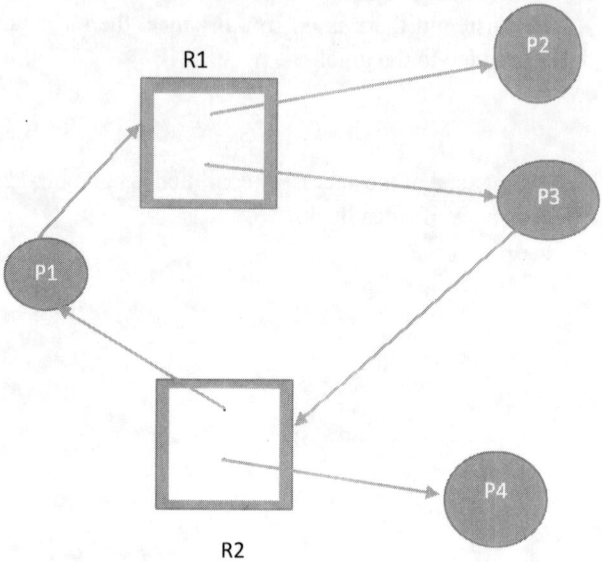

Here the cycle is formed by

P1 -> R1 -> P3 -> R2 -> P1

This is not a condition for deadlock. Process P4 can release its instance of resource type R2, and when that instance is available to P3 then the cycle can be broken.

5.4 Methods for Handling Deadlocks

There are two techniques from which we can ensure that a deadlock does not exist.

(1) Deadlock Prevention

(2) Deadlock Avoidance

Deadlock Prevention

This technique ensures that at least one of the necessary conditions does not hold true.

Deadlock Avoidance

This technique requires that beforehand additional information should be given to the operating system that which all resources the process will require and is going to use in its lifetime.

If one of the above techniques is not employed then deadlocks can occur.

5.4.1 Deadlock Prevention

By ensuring that one of the necessary condition is not met then we can prevent the occurrence of a deadlock.

5.4.1.1 Mutual Exclusion

This means that non-sharable resources should opt for mutual exclusion. That is no two processes hold a non-sharable resource at the same time. For example, a printer can cater to any one of the processes at one time. Two or more processes cannot be executing the print command at one time.

For sharable resources, mutual exclusion is not necessary. For example, a read only file is a sharable resource and two processes can access the sharable file at the same time. Here one process need not wait for the file to be released.

Deadlock cannot be prevented from occurring by only the mutual exclusion condition, since some resources by their nature are non-sharable and those resources cannot be forcibly made sharable.

5.4.1.2 Hold and Wait

The hold and wait condition should not occur together to ensure freedom from deadlock. How to prevent this is to make sure that whenever a process requests a resource, that process is not holding another resource at the same time. This can be done by the help of any one of the 3 conditions to occur.

(1) One way is to ensure that before beginning of an execution, the process requests all the resources needed and is also allocated all the resources. The system calls engaged in resource requests are done before it does any other system call.

(2) Another way is to allow a process to request for resources, if it is not having any of the resources allocated to it.

(3) Yet another way is to allow a process to request for additional resources, only if it releases all the resources, it is currently holding.

There are two disadvantages of the above:

(1) Utilisation of resources is low.

(2) It can lead to starvation.

Starvation is a condition in which a process can continually be denied of a resource to allocate to it, because that resource is always allocated to other processes before this process gets a chance to allocate.

5.4.1.3 No Pre-emption

If a process say P1 is holding some resources say R1, R2 and wants now to access a resource say R3. R3 cannot be allocated to it just now and the process has to wait for R3. In this case the resources that process P1 is holding (R1, R2) are pre-empted. This pre-emption of resources is done implicitly. The pre-empted resources (R1, R2) are added to the end of the queue of the resources that P1 is waiting for. The process P1 begins its execution again when the old resources (R1, R2) and new resources (R3) are allocated to it.

5.4.1.4 Circular Wait

This condition can be avoided by numbering all the resource types and after that each process is allowed to request for resources in increasing order of numbers.

Let R = {R1, R2, R3} be a set of resources

Each resource type is assigned a unique numerical integer. This helps to know the order of resources, which resource follows another, which is the predecessor and which is the successor.

A one to one function includes

F : R -> N

Where N is a set of integers.

Suppose we have resources R which are tape, disk drive and printer with the following integers assigned to them:

F (tape) = 1

F(disk drive) = 4

F(printer) = 11

To ensure that deadlock does not take place, we have to abide by the following protocol:

(1) A process can request for a resource type if it is in the increasing order of numbers.

$$F(Rj) > F(Ri), \text{ if } j > i$$

For example, if a process wants to access tape drive and printer at the same time, then it will have to request for tape drive first and then request for printer.

OR

(2) In case that a process is requesting an instance of resource type Rj, then that process will release any instance of resource type Ri, such that

$$F(Ri) >= F(Ri)$$

If either of these two conditions are met, then the circular wait condition cannot occur.

5.4.2 Deadlock Avoidance

The deadlock avoidance technique requires additional information as to what resources are to be requested.

There are 3 types of information required which are as follows:

(1) The resources that are currently available.

(2) The resources that are currently allocated to each process.

(3) In future what requests and releases each process would want.

The simplest model requires to know from each process how many maximum number of resources of each type it will need.

Deadlock Avoidance Algorithm

Safe State:

A Safe State is said to occur if each process is allocated its resources upto its maximum in a particular order and still avoids deadlock. Another way to describe is with the help of a safe sequence. We say a safe state exists if there is a safe sequence.

There is a sequence of processes <P1, P2…Pn> in current allocation known as a safe sequence, if

(1) For each Process Pi, the resources requested by Pi can still be offered from the currently available resources.

(2) And the resources held by other process Pj is such that j < i

If the resources that Pi requires are not available at the particular moment, then Pi should wait until Pj is completed. When Pj is finished, Pi now is in a position to get all the required resources, then Pi would complete all its work, return back all the allocated resources to the system and terminate. When Pi finishes, then Pi+1 can get all the required resources and this may continue like this.

If such a sequence does not exist, then the system is known to be in unsafe state. A safe state ensures that deadlock will not exist.

A deadlock state occurs when an unsafe state exists. All unsafe states may or may not have a deadlock. But an unsafe state can lead to a deadlock.

Example:

Let us suppose that a system has 14 magnetic tapes and 3 processes exist P1, P2 and P3.

Process P1 requires a maximum of 11 magnetic tapes

Process P2 requires a maximum of 3 magnetic tapes

Process P3 requires a maximum of 6 magnetic tapes

Suppose at this particular time T0, the following exist:

Process P1 is holding 4 magnetic tapes

Process P2 is holding 2 magnetic tapes

Process P3 is holding 3 magnetic tapes

Out of 14 magnetic tapes, 5 are free.

Process	Max need	Currently Holding
P1	11	4
P2	3	2
P3	9	3

At the time T0, the system is said to be in safe state. The sequence <P2, P1, P3> is a safe sequence. As per the discussion given below:

P2 is currently holding 2 magnetic tapes, and at maximum would want 3. So it can be allotted 1 (3-2), tape drive from the available tape drives 5.

After P2 is terminated, a total of 7 magnetic tapes are available (5 from available + 2 from releasing by P2).

After P2 has completed, P1 starts execution

P1 has a maximum need of 11 magnetic tapes, it is currently holding 4 and it can maximum ask for 7 (11-4) more. So 7 can be allotted to it since 7 are available now.

After P1 has completed, a total of 11 magnetic tapes are available (7 from available + 4 from releasing by P1).

Now P3 has to execute, according to the sequence given above.

P3 is currently holding 3 magnetic tapes and at maximum may want 6 more (9-3). So 6 can be allotted to it from 11 available. So after P3 completes, total of 14 are available (11 from available + 3 from releasing by P3).

A system may go to an unsafe state from a safe state, if for example the following takes place.

At time T0 P1 is holding 4

At time T0 P2 is holding 2

Now P3 has requested for 2 more at time T1

At time T0 P3 is holding 3

At time T1 P3 has asked 2

At time T0 requirement is (4 + 2 + 3) = 9

At time T1 requirement is = 2

Total requirement = 11

available are 14, so it is granted.

Now free after time T1 are 14 – 11 = 3

Now if sequence <P2, P1, P3> is executed then,

P2 can ask for 1 more, when it will return, we will have 5 available (3 from available + 2 from releasing by P2)

Now P1 is currently holding 4, it can ask for 7 more, but only 5 are available so it goes to an unsafe state.

Similarly, P3 is holding 3 and may ask for 6 more, but only 5 are available. So it will have to wait and therefore go in a deadlock condition.

Banker's Algorithm

Banker's Algorithm is an example of a deadlock avoidance algorithm. In this, upon entry of a new process in the system, the process is required to declare the maximum number of instances of each resource type it will need. The number of need should not exceed the total number of resources present in the system.

Upon the request of a set of resources by the user, the system is required to find out whether on allocation of these resources, the system will remain in the safe state or not.

If it will remain in safe state, then the resources are allocated, otherwise the process would have to wait until some other process releases enough number of resources.

The following data structures are required for implementation of Banker's Algorithm.

Let n be the number of processes in the system

Let m be the number of resource types.

(1) AVAILABLE – A vector of length m which tells how many number of resources of each type is available in the system at this moment.

If AVAILABLE[j] = k

This means that the resource type Rj has k number of instances available.

(2) MAX[n][m] – A double dimension matrix which tells how many number of resources of each type, each process would at the maximum ask for in the system.

If MAX[i][j] = k

This indicates for the process Pi, for the resource type Rj, k instances would at the most be asked for by process Pi.

(3) ALLOCATION[n][m] – A double dimension matrix which indicates the number of instances of each resource type is currently allocated to each process.

If ALLOCATION[i][j] = k

This indicates that k instances of resource type Rj is allocated to process Pi.

(4) NEED[n][m] – A double dimension matrix which indicates the remaining number of instances of each resource type that a process would need.

If NEED[i][j] = k

This indicates k number of instances of resource type Rj, the process Pi would need to complete its task.

Note that,

NEED[i][j] = MAX[i][j] – ALLOCATION[i][j]

If we have 2 vectors X and Y of length n then,

X <= Y if X[i] <= Y[i] for each value of i = 1,2, …n

For example, if X = (1, 6, 2, 3) and Y = (0, 5, 1, 2) then Y<=X

Each row in the matrix is for a process. If we have ALLOCATION[i] and NEED[i], then ALLOCATION [i] indicates the number of resources allocated to the process Pi.

And NEED[i] indicates that process Pi would require these many resources more to complete its task.

Safety Algorithm

This algorithm is used to find out whether a system is in a safe state or not. The algorithm is implemented as follows:

Let there be vectors WORK and FINISH of length m and n respectively.

Step 1: Set the vector WORK to same as AVAILABLE Vector.
Set FINISH Vector to FALSE, such as
FINISH[i] = FALSE for i = 1, 2,..n

Step 2: find an integer index i such that the following is true
(a) FINISH[i] ==FALSE
(b) NEED[i[<= WORK
If no such index exists, then go to Step 4

Step 3: WORK = WORK + ALLOCATION[i]
Set FINISH[i] = TRUE
Go to Step 2

Step 4: If FINISH[i] ==TRUE for all i = 1, 2, …n
Then the system is in safe state.

Let us take an example to solve this.

Suppose we have 5 processes, P1, P2, P3, P4 and P5

And 4 resources A, B, C, D

MAX

	A	B	C	D
P1	1	1	2	3
P2	2	8	6	1
P3	3	4	6	7
P4	1	7	6	3
P5	1	7	6	7

ALLOCATION

	A	B	C	D
P1	1	1	2	3
P2	2	1	1	1
P3	2	4	6	5
P4	1	7	4	3
P5	1	1	2	5

AVAILABLE

A	B	C	D
1	5	2	0

NEED

	A	B	C	D
P1	0	0	0	0
P2	1	7	5	0
P3	1	0	0	2
P4	0	0	2	0
P5	0	6	4	2

Step 1:

WORK = AVAILABLE

WORK = [1, 5, 2, 0]

FINISH[1] = FALSE

FINISH[2] = FALSE

FINISH[3] = FALSE

FINISH[4] = FALSE

FINISH[5] = FALSE

Step 2:

Find Integer, let i=1

FINISH [1] ==FALSE
NEED[1] <= WORK
[0, 0, 0, 0] <= [1, 5, 2, 0]
Both conditions true for i=1 so

Step 3:
WORK = WORK + ALLOCATION[1]
WORK = [1, 5, 2, 0] + [1, 1, 2, 3]
WORK = [2, 6, 4, 3]
FINISH[1] = TRUE
GO TO STEP 2

Step 2: Find an integer, let i=2
FINISH[2] ==FALSE
NEED[2] <= WORK
[1, 7, 5, 0] <= [2, 6, 4, 3]
Since NEED[2] not <= WORK,

so let i = 3
FINISH[3] ==FALSE
NEED[3] <= WORK
[1, 0, 0, 2] <= [2, 6, 4, 3]
Both conditions true for i=3

Step 3: WORK = WORK + ALLOCATION[3]
WORK = [2, 6, 4, 3] + [2, 4, 6, 5]
WORK= [4, 10, 10, 8]
FINISH[3] = TRUE
GO TO STEP 2

Step 2: Find an integer, let i =2
FINISH[2] == FALSE
NEED [2] <= WORK
[1, 7, 5, 0] <= [4, 10, 10, 8]
Both conditions are true for i=2

Step 3: WORK = WORK + ALLOCATION[2]
WORK = [4, 10, 10, 8] + [2, 1, 1, 1]
WORK = [6, 11, 11, 9]

FINISH[2] = TRUE

GO TO STEP 2

Step 2: Find an integer, let i = 4

FINISH[4] ==FALSE

NEED[4] <= WORK

[0, 0, 2, 0] <= [6, 11, 11, 9]

Both conditions are true for i=4

Step 3: WORK = WORK + ALLOCATION[4]

WORK = [6, 11, 11, 9] + [1, 7, 4, 3]

WORK = [7,18,15,12]

FINISH[4] = TRUE

GO TO STEP 2

Step 2:

Find an integer, let i=5

FINISH[5] ==FALSE

NEED[5] <= WORK

[0, 6, 4, 2] <= [7, 18, 15, 12]

Both conditions true for i=5

Step 3:

WORK = WORK + ALLOCATION[5]

WORK = [7, 18, 15, 12] + [1, 1, 2, 5]

WORK = [8, 19, 17, 17]

FINISH[5] = TRUE

GO TO STEP 2

Step 2: Find an integer

No more integers available,

GO TO STEP 4

Step 4:

FINISH[1] == TRUE

FINISH[2] == TRUE

FINISH[3] == TRUE

FINISH[4] == TRUE

FINISH[5] == TRUE

Then System is in safe state with the safe sequence as the order in which integers index was found.

So the safe sequence is <P1, P3, P2, P4, P5>

5.5 Deadlock Detection

Deadlocks can be detected by a wait-for-graph. The wait-for-graph algorithm can be described with the help of a resource allocation graph algorithm. We had seen that a resource allocation graph consists of two types of edges.

(1) Request Edge

(2) Assignment Edge

We introduce another type of edge called the claim edge. A claim edge goes from a process to a resource type.

Pi -> Rj

This indicates that in future at some time the process Pi would request for a resource type Rj.

The claim edge resembles a request edge in the sense that it is going from process to resource type. To distinguish between the claim edge and request edge is that claim edge is shown as dashed line and request edge is shown as a solid line.

When process Pi requests for a resource Rj. The claim edge Pi -> Rj is converted into a request edge. When a resource Rj -> Pi is released by a process Pi, the assignment edge from Rj->Pi is converted to a claim edge.

It is required that the claim would be known in advance to the system. All claim edges must be represented in the resource allocation graph before processes begin their execution.

Suppose process Pi request for a resource type Rj. In this case the request would be granted only of the conversion from a request edge Pi -> Rj to an assignment edge Rj -> Pi does not form a cycle in the resource allocation graph.

A cycle detection algorithm is used to check the safety. If the cycle does not exist then the system is said to be in a safe state. If the cycle does exist, then the system is said to be in an unsafe state. If an unsafe state exists, then the process Pi needs to wait until its request can be satisfied.

Let us consider the following graph:

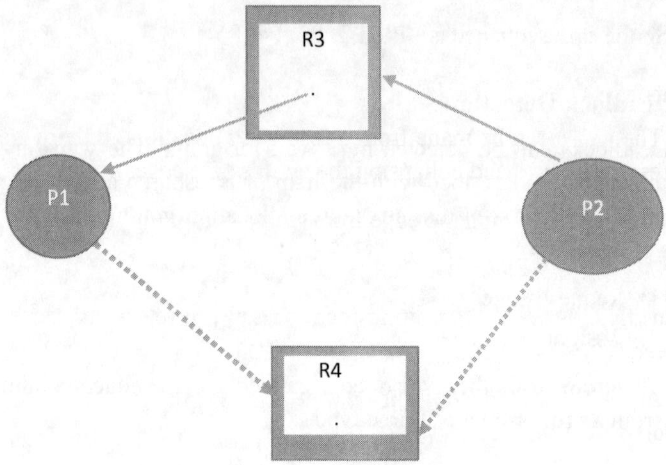

Suppose P2 is requesting for R4. It can be seen that R4 is free and can be granted to P2, but if we do that, it can be form a cycle like this.

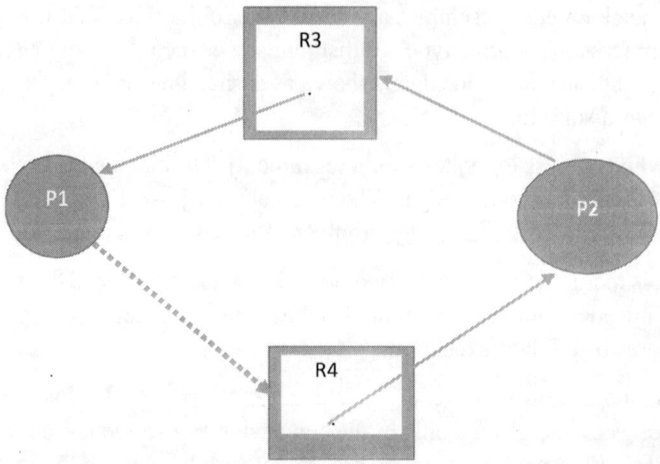

A cycle means that the system is in an unsafe state. If P1 now requests for R4, then a deadlock can occur.

Let us see how a deadlock can be detected. If the system is not ready to employ a deadlock prevention or deadlock avoidance algorithm, then a deadlock can occur.

To detect a deadlock, we need that all the resources are having a single instance of their type. With single instances, we can use a variant of resource allocation graph algorithm which is called a wait-for-graph.

Wait-for-graph

The graph can be made from a resource allocation graph by deleting the resource nodes and collapsing the appropriate edges.

In a wait-for-graph the edge from

Pi -> Pj

means that process Pi is waiting for process Pj to release a resource that Pi needs.

An edge Pi-> Pj will exist in the wait-for-graph only if the corresponding resource allocation graph has

Pi -> Rk and Rk -> Pj

for a resource type Rk.

Consider the following diagram:

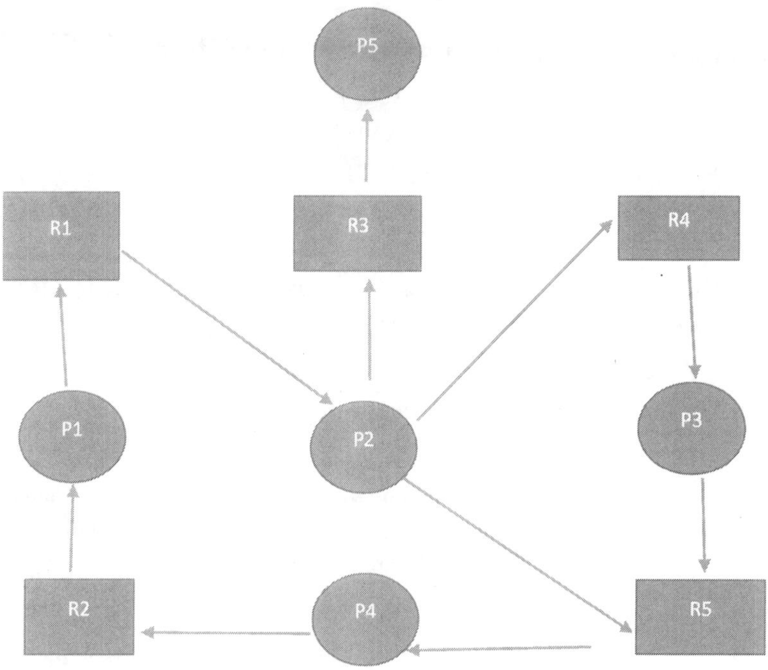

Wait-for-graph is obtained by removing the resource nodes.

An edge Pi -> Pj exists

If process Pi is waiting for Pj to release some resource that Pi needs.

So we can see

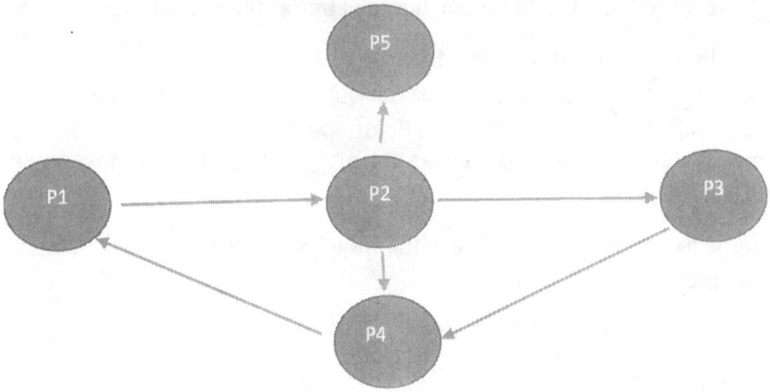

P1 -> P2	SINCE P1->R1 AND R1 -> P2 IS THERE
P2->P3	SINCE P2->R4 AND R4-> P3 IS THERE
P3->P4	SINCE P3->R5 AND R5 -> P4 IS THERE
P4-> P1	SINCE P4-> R1 AND R1 -> P1 IS THERE
P2 -> P5	SINCE P2 -> R3 AND R3-> P5 IS THERE
P2-> P4	SINCE P2-> R5 AND R5-> P4 IS THERE

5.6 Recovery from Deadlock

Once we have learnt that a deadlock is existing, we can recover from deadlock by the following alternatives:

(1) Abort one or more processes to break circular wait

(2) Pre-empt the resources held by deadlocked processes

(1) Process Abortion:

This can be done by one of the following methods, in either case the system will get back all the resources which the deadlocked processes are holding.

(a) Abortion of All Deadlocked Processes:

This breaks the deadlocked cycle, but at the cost of great

extent. The deadlocked processes could be completed long back and the partial computation need to be discarded and re-computations have to be done later on.

(b) Abortion of one process at a time until the deadlock is broken:

Again this has a costly overhead, as after the abortion of each process, we need to check with a deadlock detection algorithm whether some processes are still deadlocked.

To abort a process is not that easy. Suppose that the process was in the middle of updating a file, then termination of the process would lead to the file be in an incorrect state.

And if we use the partial termination technique, then we need to find out whether deadlocked process (or processes) need to be terminated. The termination should be done at the lowest cost.

Lowest cost can be based on:

(1) The priority of the process

(2) How long has the process executed, and how much more time does it need for completion of its task.

(3) The type of resources that the process is using. Can those processes be easily pre-empted.

(4) How many more number of resources the process needs to complete its task.

(5) How many processes need to be terminated.

(6) Whether it is an interactive process or batch.

(2) Resource Pre-emption

Deletion of deadlocks with the help of pre-emption of resources requires us to pre-empt some resources from processes and provide those resources to other processes in the system. For pre-emption of resources to take place, the following should be considered:

(1) Selecting a Victim:

We need to find out which processes and which resources are to be pre-empted. Here we need to take care of the cost on the basis of 2 factors

(a) The no. of resources that a deadlocked process is holding

(b) The amount of time that the process has this far consumed during its execution.

(2) Rollback:

If we are pre-empting a resource from a process, then that process would need to rollback, because it cannot continue any further with normal execution. The rollback has to be done to a point where a system is in a safe state. A safe state is usually difficult to determine, therefore a total rollback is required, and the process has to be restarted.

(3) Starvation:

If the resources of the same process are always being pre-empted, then that process would never be able to execute. So before selecting a process for pre-emption, we would need to find out how we should select our victim.

The same process is always picked up for pre-emption every time. To ensure that this does not happen, we see that the process is pre-empted only for a finite number of value. To determine the finite number, we can count the number of rollbacks the process has gone through.

Chapter - 6

Memory Management

6.1 Introduction

Memory needs to be shared if we want to increase CPU utilisation. There are a number of memory management algorithms which vary from a primitive bare machine to paging and segmentation. These algorithms need to check whether h/w is supportive enough to cater to these techniques. Memory is made of a large array of words or bytes and it is byte addressable. CPU is used to fetch instructions from the memory according to the value in the program counter. These instructions may need to load or store from the memory area. An instruction execution cycle works as follows:

First an instruction is fetched from the memory. The instruction is further decoded and may require more operands to be fetched from the memory area. After the successful execution of the instruction, the results that it had calculated may need to be stored back in memory area. Memory Unit sees only a stream of memory addresses without knowing how they were generated.

The Basic Structure

The CPU directly accesses only the main memory (RAM) or the CPU registers available to it. Some machine instructions do require to pass memory addresses as arguments. If suppose that the data is not present in the memory at the moment, then the data would need to be moved into the area before CPU begins its execution.

When data is fetched from CPU registers, it is more faster than accessing from the RAM. Fetching data from RAM takes may clock cycles. So here a cache is needed. A cache is a fast memory between the CPU and RAM. Each process is given its own separate memory space. So each process has a set of legal addresses for it to execute. We need to make sure that the process accesses only its legal addresses. This is done with the help of 2 registers:

1) BASE
2) LIMIT

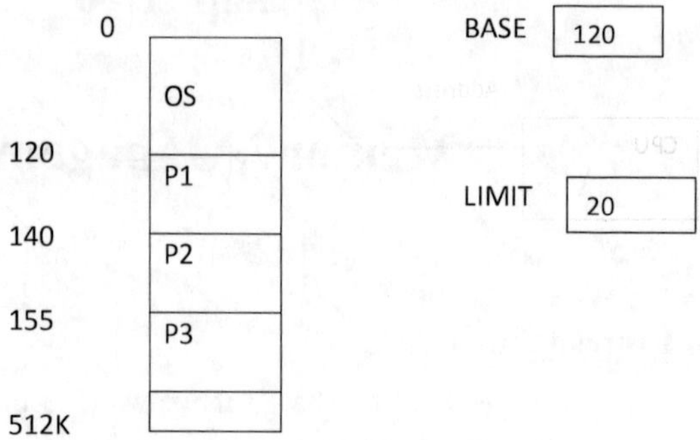

LOGICAL ADDRESS SPACE

Each program has its own base and limit values, which can be populated in the registers. The BASE holds the smallest legal physical memory address that the program can access and LIMIT stores the length of the program. So that program can access memory area between its BASE and LIMIT values. Suppose for program P1, the BASE address is 120 and the LIMIT is 20, then that program can access memory area from 120 to 139 (inclusive).

To ensure that the program is accessing only its legal address space, a h/w comparison is required for every address generated by the user to the BASE and LIMIT registers. If the program is trying to access a memory area which stores the operating system or some other program's memory area, then a fault is generated by the operating system and this attempt is known as fatal error.

The values in the BASE and LIMIT registers are populated only by the operating system using special privileged instructions. These privileged instructions are executed only in the kernel mode. Only operating system can execute kernel level instructions. So only operating system can load values in the BASE and LIMIT registers. OS does prevent user program to change the contents of these registers. The OS which is executing in kernel mode can access the memory area assigned to kernel and memory area assigned to user. So it is the responsibility of OS to load User's program in user's memory area.

If we access another process's memory area then a fatal error will occur as shown in the diagram below.

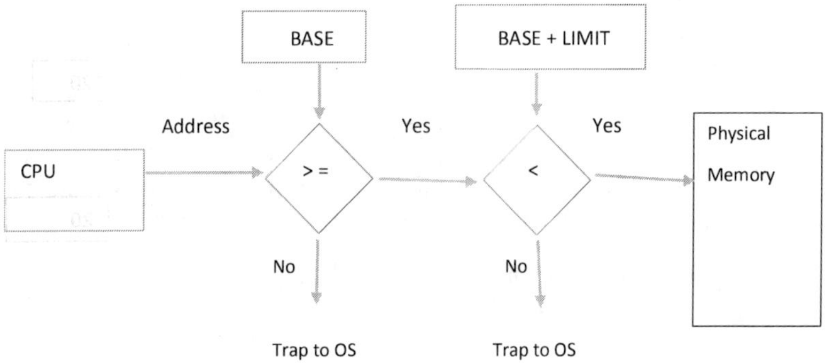

Logical and Physical Address Space

An address generated by the CPU is known as the logical address. And the address which the memory unit deals with is the physical address space, this address is loaded in the MAR register.

During compile time address binding and load time address binding, the physical address and logical address are identical. Whereas during execution time address binding, the physical and logical addresses differ.

Logical addresses are also known as Virtual Addresses. The logical address which are generated by the program fall in logical address space. And the set of physical addresses which correspond to these logical addresses fall in physical address space.

The Memory Management Unit (MMU) is responsible for mapping virtual address to physical address during runtime. The BASE register is now known as relocation register. Each address generated by the user program is added to the relocation register and then sent to memory for access.

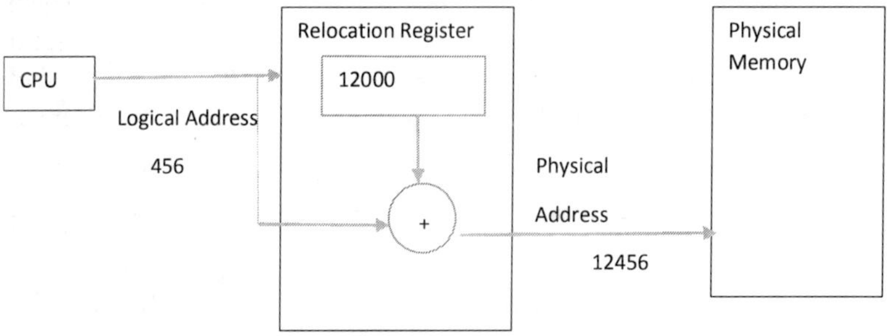

If the BASE register has a value 12000, then when the user tries to access address 0. It is dynamically relocated to location 12000. And if it tries to access address 456, then it will be relocated to 12456.

6.2 Swapping

A process must reside in the Main Memory (RAM) for execution. A process which is executing in RAM can be picked and put in the secondary memory (Disk). Similarly that program can be picked from secondary memory and put in the RAM for execution.

This process of taking out is known as Swapping. A process is said to Swap In, if it is brought into the RAM and Swap Out if it is taken out of RAM.

Consider the Round Robin Algorithm in multiprogramming environment. On the expiration of a time slice, the memory manager swaps that process out of the RAM and brings in another process into the RAM from secondary storage for execution next. In this time the CPU scheduler allocates a time slice to another process.

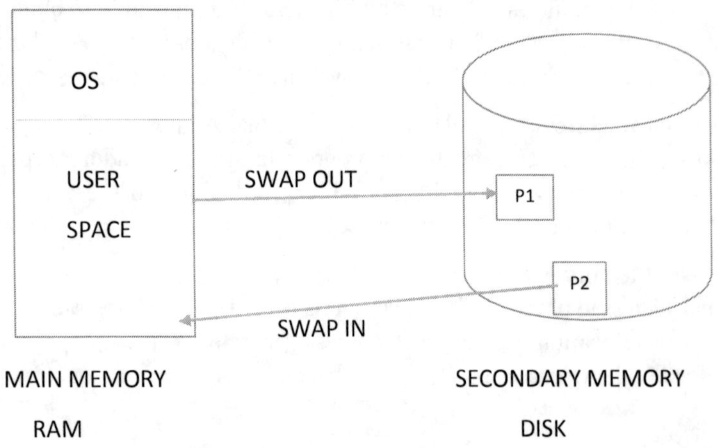

When all time slices of all processes have expired, then some other process is swapped in for continued execution.

Consider priority based scheduling. Whenever a higher priority process arrives and needs execution, then the memory manager would do the following:

swap out lower priority process,

load higher priority and
starts execution.

On the completion of a higher priority, the lower priority process can then be swapped in and continue execution. A ready queue is maintained for those processes which want CPU for execution. The scheduler invokes the dispatcher when it has decided to execute a process. The dispatcher sees that the process ready for execution is placed at the head of the ready queue. If it is not present in the ready queue and no memory is available in RAM. Then it will swap out some other process currently in RAM and Swap in a desired process. The registers are loaded and control given to allocated process. The context switching time in swapping is very much higher.

6.3 Contiguous Memory Allocation

The main memory (RAM) consists of 2 main contents:

(1) Part of the Operating System which is sufficient enough for executing current task. If some other task requires some other part of the operating system then that part of operating system is brought into the RAM.

(2) The various user processes, ready for execution.

Therefore, we need to organise main memory in an efficient manner. The contiguous memory has 2 partitions as described above.

(1) Resident Operating system

(2) User processes

The OS is placed either in the low memory or high memory. An interrupt vector affects the location of the above 2. Most of the time the interrupt vector is placed in low memory. Then in that case the operating system is also placed in low memory area.

The user wants many processes to be placed in the RAM at the same time. Therefore the user wants to know how to allocate available memory to processes which are waiting in the ready queue to be brought into the RAM.

In contiguous memory allocation scheme, each process gets a single contiguous section of memory.

6.4 Memory Mapping and Protection

The smallest physical address is stored in the relocation register. The range of logical addresses is stored in the LIMIT register.

Let us take an example and have values as follows:

RELOCATION register = 100
LIMIT register = 76

Taking the relocation register and the limit register, each logical address needs to be less than the limit register.

The logical addresses are mapped dynamically by adding the value to the relocation register. The MMU is responsible for doing this

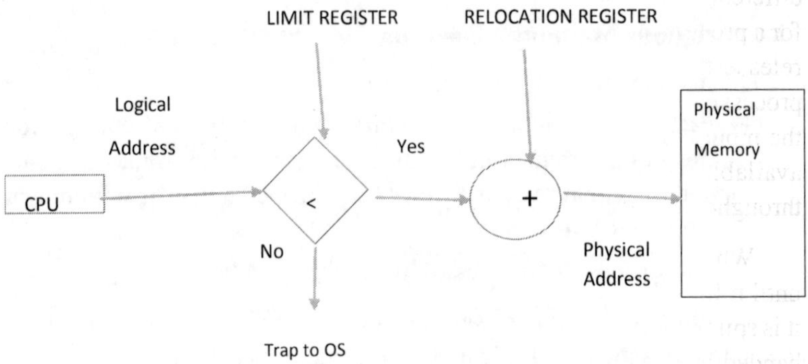

The mapped address is sent to memory.

When a process is selected by the CPU scheduler for execution, then it is the responsibility of the dispatcher to load the relocation register and the limit register as part of context switching. The logical address generated by the CPU is checked with the values of these registers. It is also taken care that the Operating System space and other users space is not modified by this process.

Memory Allocation

How should the memory be allocated. The easiest way to allocate memory is to divide the memory into fixed sized partitions. And each partition has one process to contain. Therefore, the number of programs would be equal to the number of partitions and this then becomes the degree of multiprogramming.

In this multiple partition scheme, as a partition becomes free, a process can be loaded in it from the ready queue. As soon as the process terminates, its partition is free and other processes can utilised the freed partition space. This commonly occurs in Batch Processing environment.

Variable Partition Method

In a variable partition method, the operating system has a table which indicates which parts of memory are available and which are occupied. In the beginning the memory is one big chunk of available space known as a hole so that user processes can utilise it. Later on the memory contains holes of different sizes. At any point of time a list of available holes and an input queue is there for reference. Memory gets allocated to processes of different sizes until it may happen that no more big enough space is available for a process to fit in. The operating system then has to wait until processes release their partitions and a big enough hole becomes available for processing. The other thing that operating system can do is to travel down the input queue to find out if any process is small enough and can fit in available space right now. The holes of different sizes are scattered throughout the memory area.

When a process comes for execution, it searches the memory area until it finds a hole big enough to cater it. If the hole is large enough, then it is spilt into two parts. One part is allocated to the process and the other is handed over to the list of holes. On termination of a process, its block of memory is released and placed with the list of other holes. If a hole is right next to another hole, then they are merged to form a bigger hole. The operating system then checks if there is any process waiting for a big hole to be available and so the process gets allocated.

This is known as dynamic storage allocation which can be implemented with any of the three methods:

(1) First Fit

(2) Best Fit

(3) Worst Fit

(1) First Fit: This allocates the first hole that is big enough. The search stops as soon as the operating system finds a free hole which is big enough for the process. Searching generally starts at the beginning of the set of holes or at the point where the previous first fit search had stopped.

(2) Best Fit: This allocates the smallest hole that is big enough. The entire list needs to be searched if the list is not sorted by size. This method produces the smallest leftover holes.

(3) Worst Fit: The largest hole is allocated. This also requires that the entire list is to be searched to find the biggest hole available. If the list is sorted by size, then entire list need not be searched. This method produces the largest leftover hole. In this case, it may benefit that larger leftover holes may accommodate processes.

Looking at the time and storage utilisation, it is observed that Best Fit and First Fit perform better than Worst Fit.

(1) Consider First Fit:

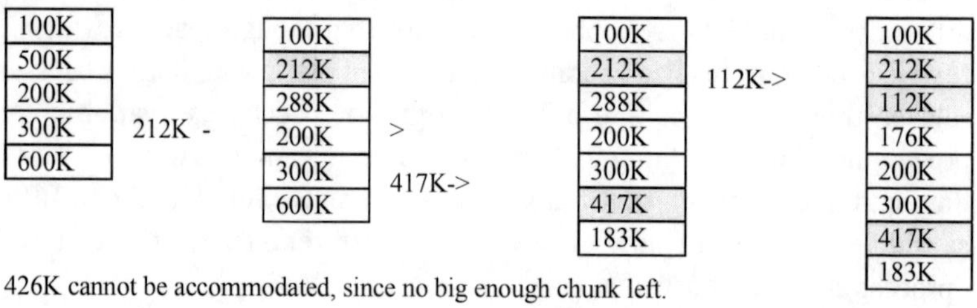

426K cannot be accommodated, since no big enough chunk left.

426 will be accommodated if we combine 200k and 300k

Consider Best Fit:

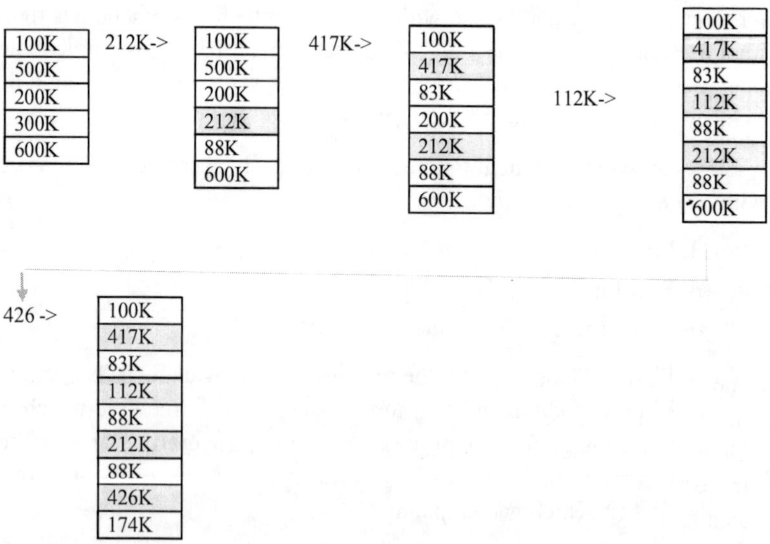

Let us take an example to understand the above methods. Consider a memory partition of 100K, 500K, 200K, 300K and 600K (in this order). How would each of the First Fit, Best Fit and Worst Fit algorithms place processes of 212K, 417K, 112K and 426K (in this order). Also which algorithm is makes the most efficient use of memory.

(2) Consider Worst Fit:

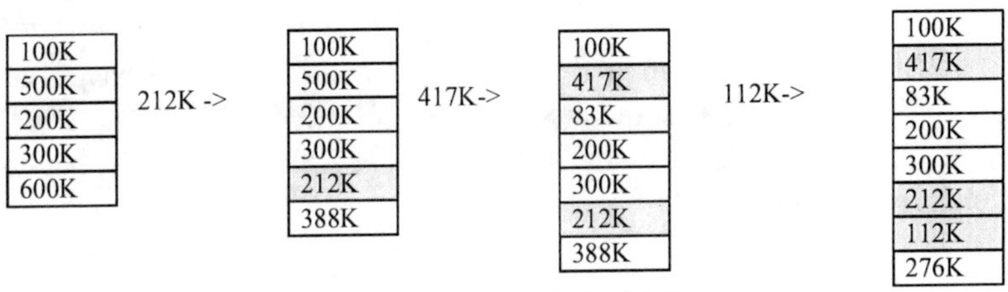

426K cannot be accommodated, since no big enough chunk left.

426 will be accommodated if we do combine 200k and 300k

6.5 Fragmentation

All the above mentioned strategies have external fragmentation. The processes are put in the memory and later they release the occupied memory. So this forms little broken pieces of memory here and there.

We define external fragmentation as the amount of space needed by a process is available, the only difference is that it is not contiguous. The broken pieces are interleaved with memory occupied by other processes. The storage space is said to be fragmented into a large number of small holes.

The worst condition occurs if every 2 processes have a hole between themselves. If all the broken pieces were accumulated and formed one big hole, then we would be able to cater to many processes.

In comparison to external fragmentation. There can also be internal fragmentation. If we have a multiple partition allocation scheme with a hole big enough as 16,242 bytes and a process requests for 16,240 bytes. If this process is allocated to the available block, 2 bytes would go wasted. And the overhead of keeping track of 2 bytes available would be huge enough than the hole itself. To avoid this problem, we divide the physical memory into fixed sized blocks and memory is allocated in terms of the blocks. In this case the memory allocated to a process would be slightly more than the requested memory. The unused memory in blocks is known as internal fragmentation.

Compaction

To address the problem of external fragmentation is compaction. Compaction is done by combining all the unused memory together as a single block. The easy way out to this is to move all processes to one end of the memory and to keep all holes together at the other end of memory making a big hole. Now this is very difficult to do and quite expensive in the cost of going re-arrangement.

Consider the following area of physical memory. In this we have holes of 100K, 83K, 88K, 88K and 74K. If a process arrives which needs 200K, then it cannot be allocated anywhere, as we see 200K is available, but not adjacent to each other.

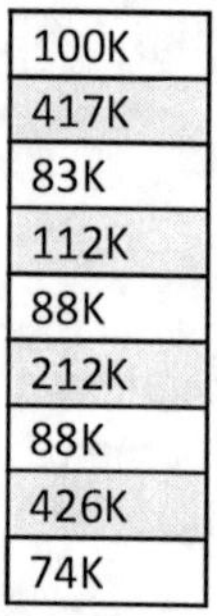

By doing Compaction, shifting free holes at the lower end of memory and shifting the used memory to the upper end of memory, the physical memory will look like this:

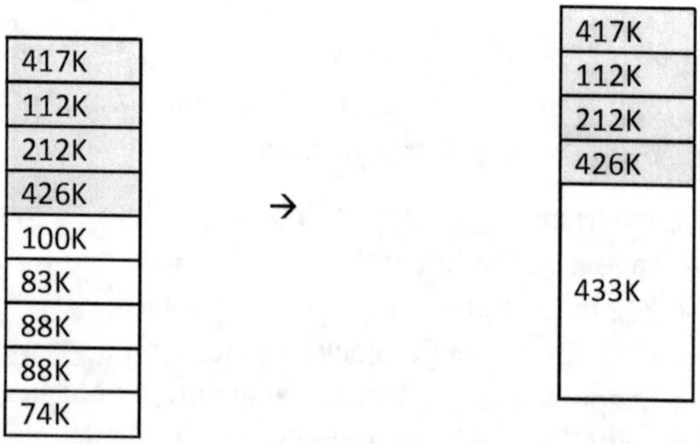

Now we can allocate 200K to the process desiring it as we can see that we have a chunk of 433K available, but the cost of movement of memory blocks is too high.

The solution to the above problem is to make logical address space of a program non-contiguous. In this case wherever the memory is available, it can be provided to a process. This is done by any one of the two methods:

(1) Paging

(2) Segmentation

6.6 Paging

Paging allows for the physical address space to be non-contiguous for a process. Paging helps in avoiding External fragmentation and Compaction.

How is paging done?

The physical memory is divided into fixed sized partitions which are known as frames. The logical memory is also divided into the same fixed sized partitions known as pages. On the execution of a process, the pages are taken from the disk drive and loaded into any frame which is empty in the physical memory. The disk itself is divided into the same sized partitions or blocks and they are of the same size as the frames.

The logical address that the CPU generates consists of two parts:

(1) A page number (p)

(2) A page offset (d)

The page number gives an index into a page table. The function of the page table is to contain the base address of each page in the physical memory. Along with the page's base address the page offset is added to generate the physical address of the memory. This address is then sent to fetch the contents from the physical memory

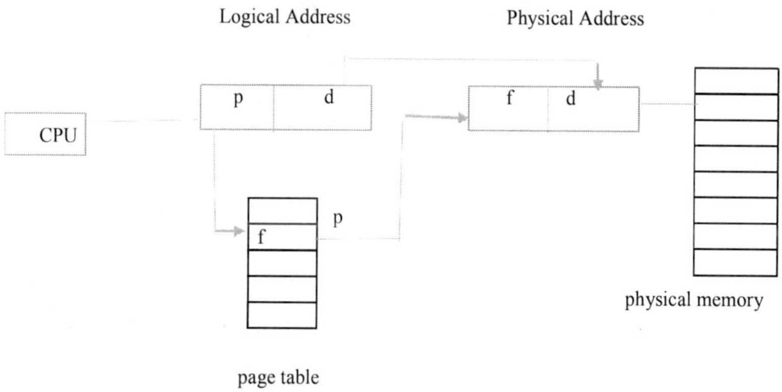

Suppose we have the following:

Page No.
page 0
page 1
page 2
page 3

Logical Memory

	Frame No.
0	1
1	6
2	3
3	7

Page Table

	Frame No.
0	
1	page 0
2	
3	page 2
4	
5	
6	page 1
7	page 3

Physical Memory

The page size, the frame size is defined by the h/w. The size of page is generally kept as a power of 2. This can range from 512 bytes to 16MB per page.

In case the logical address space is 2^m and page size is 2^n, then m-n bits of the logical space distinguish the page number. And the low order n bits designate the page offset as the displacement within the page.

Consider the following example

If n=2 and m=4

Then Logical Memory = $2^m = 2^4 = 16$ bytes

Let Physical Memory be $2^5 = 32$ bytes

Page Size = $2^n = 2^2 = 4$ bytes

Then total number of bits in logical memory to distinguish page number $= m - n = 4 - 2 = 2$

With 2 bits we can have the following combinations

00

01

10

11

Total number of pages = 4

Total number of offset within a page = n = 2

So with 2 bits, we can have the following combinations within an offset.

00

01

10

11

Total number of offsets within a page = 4

page no.	page offset
p	d
m-n	n

Page No.	Position	
0	0	I
	1	J
	2	K
	3	L
1	4	M
	5	N
	6	O
	7	P
2	8	Q
	9	R
	10	S
	11	T
3	12	U
	13	V
	14	W
	15	X

Logical Memory

Page No.	Frame No.
0	7
1	2
2	4
3	1

Page Table

Frame	position No.	
0	0	
	1	
	2	
	3	
1	4	u
	5	v
	6	w
	7	x
2	8	m
	9	n
	10	o
	11	p
3	12	
	13	
	14	
	15	
4	16	q
	17	r
	18	s
	19	t
5	20	
	21	
	22	
	23	
6	24	
	25	
	26	
	27	
7	28	i
	29	j
	30	k
	31	l

Physical Memory

The logical address 0 is at Page 0 and offset 0 (content: i)

So page 0 is in frame 7 as per page table.

Physical address $= 7 \times 4 + 0$

$= 28$

Logical address 3 is in page 0 offset 3 (content: u)

So page 0 is in frame 7 offset 3

Physical Address $= 7 \times 4 + 3$

$= 28 + 3$

$= 31$

Logical address 4 is in page 1 offset 0 (content: m)

So page 1 is in frame 2 offset 0

Physical Address $= 2 \times 4 + 0$

$= 8$

Logical Address 13 is in page 3 offset 1 (content: v)

So page 3 is in frame 1 offset 1

Physical Address $= 1 \times 4 + 1$

$= 4 + 1$

$= 5$

Internal Fragmentation

Paging is free from external fragmentation. The process requires certain pages and those are placed in the frames. If the length of the process is not fitting entirely in frames, then the last allocated frame may have some amount of memory left. It will happen because the memory requirements of a process may not coincide with page boundaries. The last frame allocated might not be full. The left out memory is known as internal fragmentation.

For example, let us assume that the page size is 512 bytes. Suppose a process needs 1122 bytes. So this will require 3 frames of 512 bytes. The first frame will hold 512 bytes, the second frame will also hold 512 bytes and the third frame will hold 98 bytes (1122- (512*2)). Now since the page size is of 512 bytes and only 98 bytes are required. So 414 bytes (512-98) will not be used of the third frame and these will go waste. Since a new process would require a fresh frame. So we say that internal fragmentation of 414 bytes has occurred.

Translation Lookaside Buffer

The page table has large number of entries around upto 1 million. To speed up the process of extraction of a frame number we have a small fast lookup h/w cache which is known as translation lookaside buffer (TLB).

The TLB is a fast memory which is composed of 2 fields:

(1) A Key (or Tag)

(2) A Value

The TLB uses the concept of associative memory. An associative memory means that all entries are compared at the same time to make it fast.

When the item is found, its corresponding value field is retrieved, which is the frame number. The h/w cache is very fast but very expensive at the same time. The memory size of TLB is relatively small varying between 64 and 1024.

The TLB can be used with page tables as follows:

A TLB would contain a limited number of page table entries. When the CPU generates a logical address. The page number is presented to the TLB. If the page number is found, its corresponding frame number is immediately made available to access the physical memory.

If the page number is not in the TLB (then it is called a TLB miss) and if the page number is found in the TLB (then it is called a TLB hit). In case of a TLB miss, we need to go the page table and access the desired frame number. And this frame number will be used to access the physical memory.

The combination of page number and frame number found recently in the page table is added to the TLB so that for future references they can be accessed from the TLB instead of the page table.

The percentage of times that a particular page number is found in the TLB is known as the hit ratio. A percentage of 80 as a hit ratio means that the page number is found in the TLB 80% of the time.

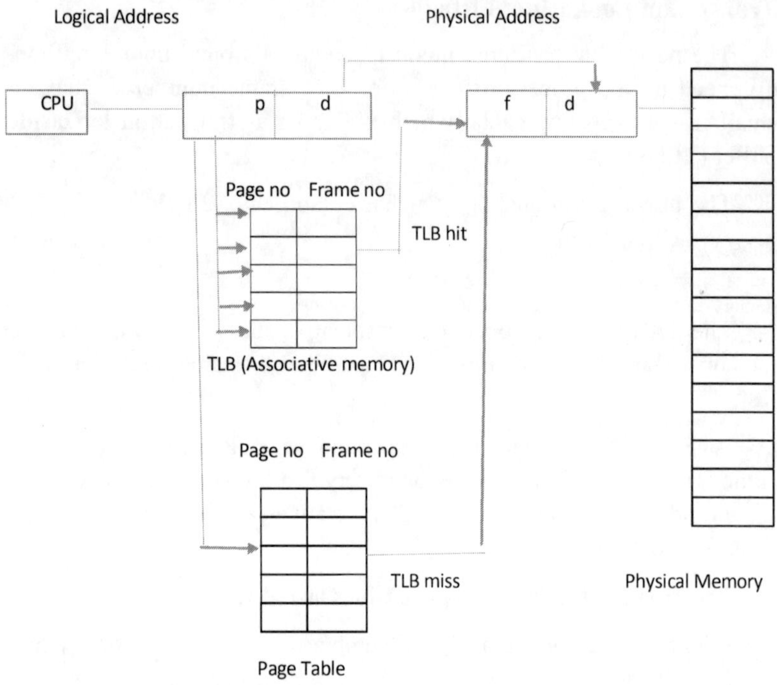

Protection

In a paged oriented environment, the protection is done with the help of protection bits associated with each frame. These bits are normally kept in the page table. A bit can define a page to be read/write or read only page. The references to the physical memory are done via the page table to acquire the correct frame number.

When the physical address is being computed, the protection bits can be checked to verify that no writes are being made to the read only page. Another special bit is associated with the page table, which is known as valid/invalid bit. When the bit is set to "valid" it means that the page exists in the process's logical address space and if the bit is set to invalid, it means that page number is not in the process's logical address space. Let us take an example to demonstrate it. Suppose we have a system with 12 bit address space, i.e. 2^{12} addresses or 4096 addresses. Suppose a process requires addresses from 0 to 2298.

If we have page size of 1KB, then we have,

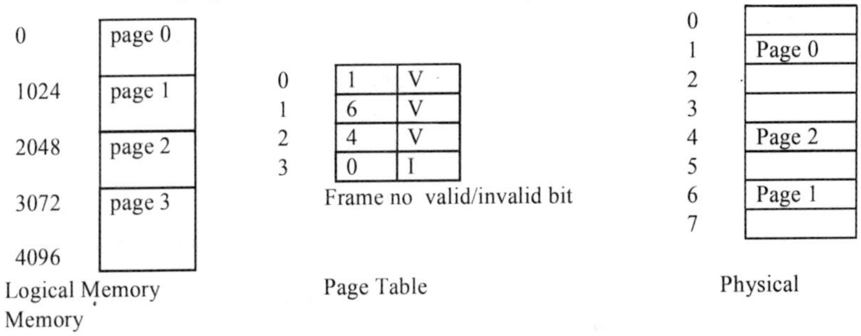

The addresses in pages 0, 1, 2 are mapped normally through the page table. The attempt to generate an address in page 3 is invalid as is shown by invalid bit. The program has a valid logical address space from 0 to 2298, any reference beyond that is illegal. So program extends to the address space of 2298. Any reference beyond that is illegal but since page 2 is active then the addresses from 2048 to 3072 are valid. Any address which lies in page 3 that is from 3073 to 4096 is invalid. So an internal fragmentation occurs in page 2.

6.7 Segmentation

Paging does not allow us to get the user's view of memory. Segmentation allows us to get the user's view of memory. User's view consists of segments. Segments may have functions, procedures and methods. It may also consist of data structures, objects, arrays, stacks and variables. It may also consist of main program or a math library. The order of appearance of these segments does not make a difference. A stack may be placed before a function or equally after a function. The length of the segments are of variable length. The length of the segment is dependent on the purpose of the segment in the program. The segments have offsets to represent their elements starting from the base address of the segment. Example, the first statement of the program, the sixth entry in the stack, the 2nd instruction of a sum() function. Segmentation is another kind of memory management scheme which supports the user's view of memory. The logical address space in segmentation is the space which is occupied by segments. Each segment has a name and length associated with it. The address now consists of segment name and the offset within the segment. The address field needs to have the following values supplied to it:

(1) The name of segment

(2) And an offset

To achieve simplicity, segments are numbered and instead of the name of the segment, the number of the segment is specified in the address.

So the logical address consists of <segment number, offset>

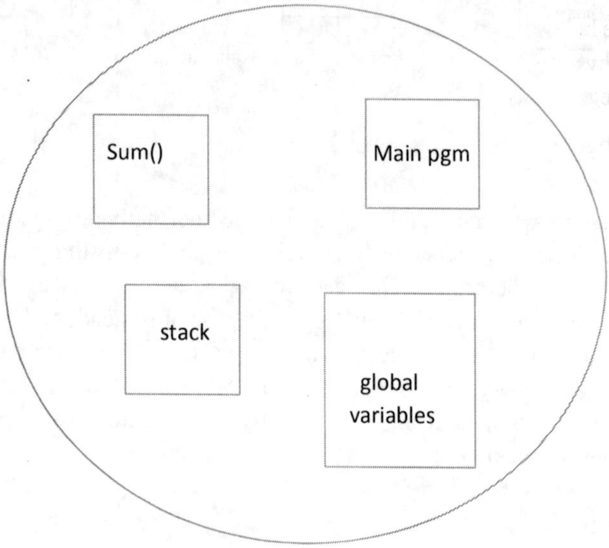

The h/w in segmentation consists of the following:

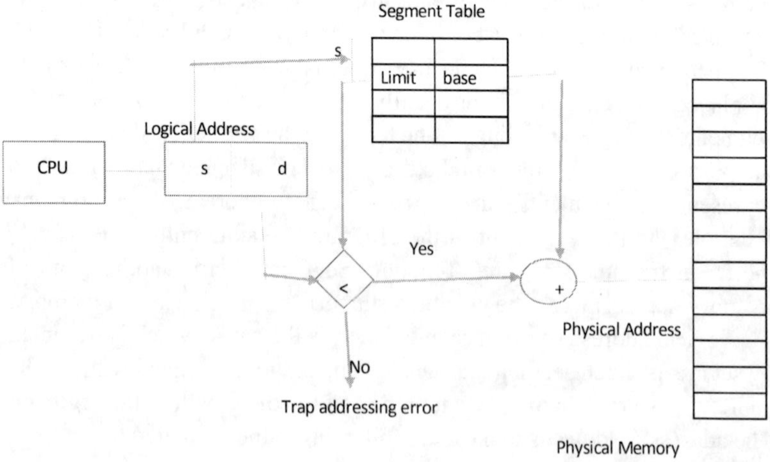

The logical address that is the < segment number, offset > must be mapped to the physical address in the memory. This mapping is done with the help of a segment table. The segment table entries consist of 2 fields:

(1) The segment base address, (2) The offset

The base of the segment consists of the starting address of the segment in the physical memory. The limit of a segment basically means the length of the segment.

A logical address consists of 2 parts:

(1) a segment number (s) (2) an offset into the segment (d)

The segment number (s) is the index in the segment table. The offset number (d) should lie between 0 and the segment limit.

If the offset (d) is beyond the limit of the segment, then a system error occurs in the operating system and the fetching of the physical address cannot be continued.

When the value of offset is correct, then base address of the segment is added to the offset to fetch the physical address from the memory.

The segment table consist of the number of entries as many as the number of segments there exist. Each segment entry consists of a pair of base and the limit values for that particular segment.

Consider the following figure:

User's View

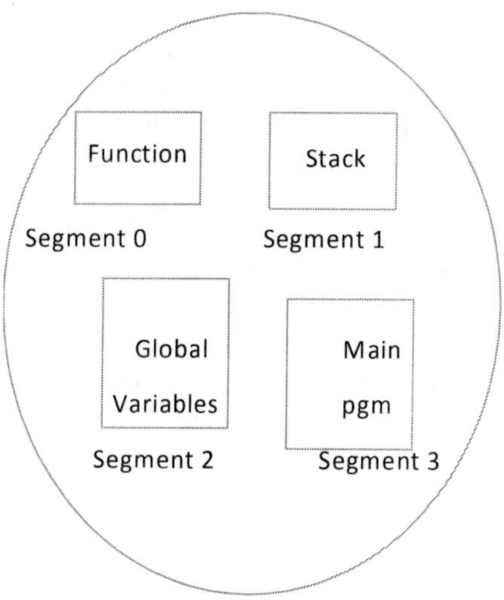

Segment Table

	Limit	Base
0	500	1200
1	200	1800
2	600	2800
3	1000	4000

Here we have 4 segments numbered 0 to 3. For each segment, there is a separate entry in the segment table. The entry consists of the base address of that segment in the physical memory and the length of that segment or its limit.

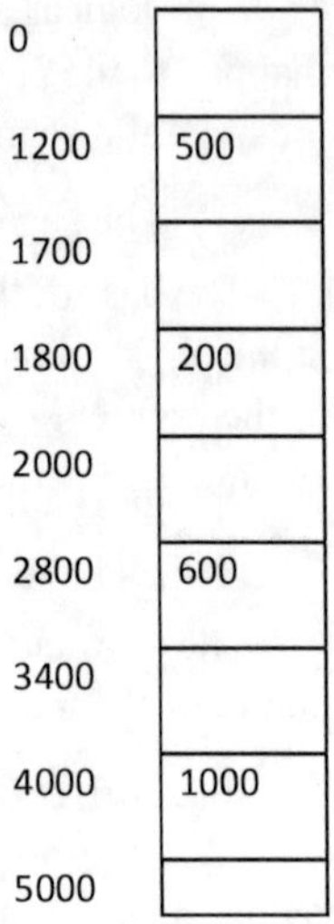

Let us take an example from the above figure:

Suppose segment 2 has a base address of 2800 and its length or offset of 600. Thus, a reference to the byte 152 of segment 2 will be mapped to the physical address location:

2800 + 152 = 2952

A reference to segment 3 byte 54 will be mapped to the physical address location:

4000 + 54 = 4054

A reference to byte 1255 of segment 3 will result to a trap in the operating system as segment 3 is only 1000 bytes long and its limit is set to 1000. So the comparison of offset < limit will be false (1255 < 1000).

Paged Segmentation

Paged Segmentation uses the concept of paging and segmentation both.

The logical address consists of <s, p, d> where s is the segment number or an index into the segment table. Each segment has a page table associated with it. The p indicates the page number in the page table which is associated with that segment. The d indicates the offset within the page.

s is an index in the segment table, p is an index into page table. Segment table entry of s gives us the base address of the page table associated with that segment. The page table base address is combined with the p to get to the desired entry in the page table or to get to the desired page. The page is used to get the desired frame number. Each page table entry has an associated frame number with it. The frame number together with the offset d is used to get to the desired physical address in the physical memory.

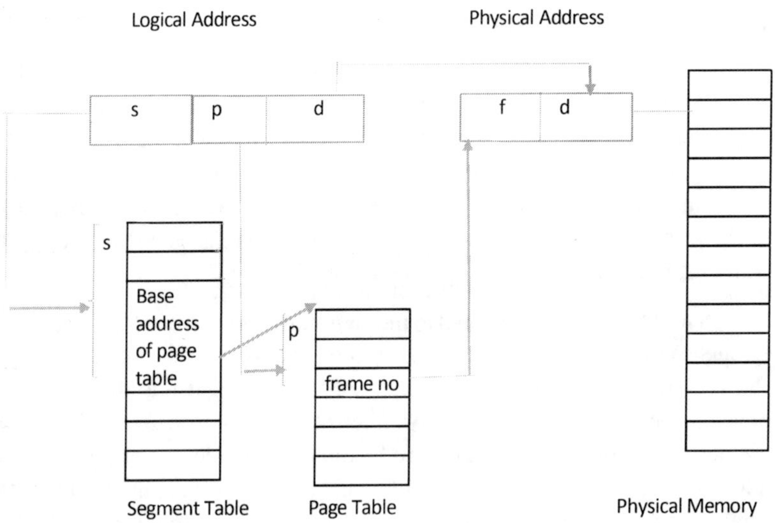

In a paged segmented system, a virtual address consists of 32 bits of which 12 bits are for displacement, 11 bits are segment number and 9 bits are page number. Calculate the following:

(a) Page Size
(b) Maximum Segment Size
(c) Maximum Number of Pages
(d) Maximum Number of Segments

Let s denote the segment number
Let p denote the page number
Let d denote the displacement

S	p	d
11 bits	9 bits	12 bits

(a) Page Size = 2^n where n is the displacement or offset within a page
$= 2^{12}$

(b) Maximum Segment Size = $2^9 \times * 2^{12}$

(c) Maximum Number of Pages = $2^{11} \times * 2^9$

(d) Maximum Number of Segments = 2^{11}

6.8 Virtual Memory Management

To achieve multiprogramming the memory needs to have multiple programs to be present in it at the same time. Also to run a process, all of its contents should be present in the memory. With the help of virtual memory, we can ensure that the whole process is not required to be present in the memory at the same time. The programs may be larger than the RAM or the physical memory. Most of the time, there is no need to have an entire program in the memory for execution.

As an example, there may be a situation in which the code to handle erroneous condition is not required in the process. So that piece of code can very well lie in the secondary memory and brought into the RAM or physical memory if it is required. Another situation may occur in allocating memory to array, lists and tables. To be on the safe side, the program may allocate larger memory to those elements, such as allocating a 100×100 array when only a 20×20 is required. Also to set a symbol table to 1000 when only 200 symbols are required.

Even if entire program is needed, it may be so that all of it is not needed at the time. A partial program in memory can get us many benefits. Therefore, a big program which is larger than the size of the RAM can also be executed. A lot of virtual space can also be used thereby simplifying the programming task. As the user programs would need less physical space, more programs will be able to run at the same time. The less I/O would be needed for swapping programs in and out of the RAM, thereby increasing the speed of processes to run faster.

Virtual Memory

The virtual memory is the logical memory which is different than the physical memory. As a result, a large chunk of virtual memory can be provided to users when very little amount of physical memory is available. This allows the users not to worry about the program size being fitted into the physical memory and can concentrate on writing programs.

Virtual Address Space

This is a view of how the memory of a process is organised. The view can be depicted as follows:

Suppose a process begins at the memory address 0 in case of a contiguous memory allocation as shown below:

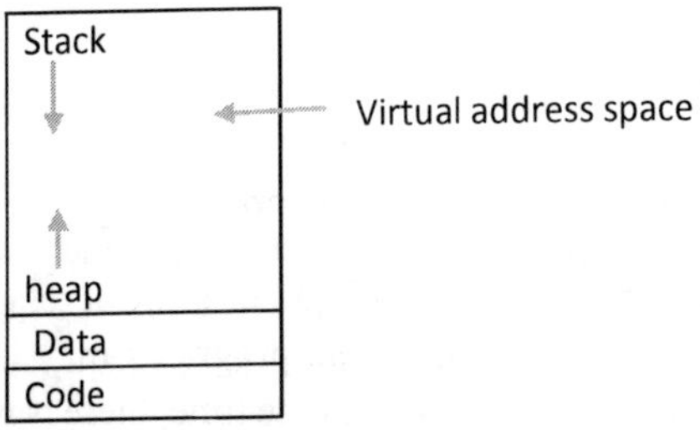

For dynamic memory allocation, we do not require all the pages to be present in the virtual address space at the same time. The stack grows in downward direction and the heap grows in upward direction, so the space left between the two is the virtual address space which is dynamic in nature.

6.9 Demand Paging

We need not load the whole program into RAM at the same time since all of it may not be required at the same time. So as an alternative, we use pages to be loaded into RAM as and when they are required. The concept is known as demand paging and is used with virtual memory systems. In a demand paged virtual memory, pages will be loaded when they are demanded during the execution of a program. The pages which are not required by the process during its execution are never demanded and thus never loaded into RAM and they remain on the disk all the time.

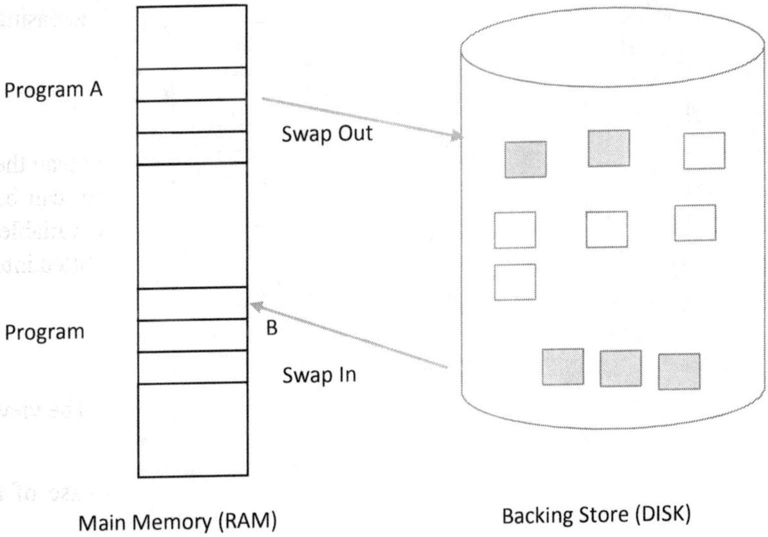

A demand paging system can be compared to the paging system. In which swapping takes place between the process which are lying on the secondary memory (i.e. disk). Whenever we need to execute a process, it is swapped into the RAM. Instead of swapping the whole process into the RAM at the beginning of the process, we use a technique that is known as the lazy swapper. A lazy swapper would swap a page into the RAM only when that page is required by the process. Now the process is perceived as a sequence of pages.

Whenever there is a need of some pages required by the process, they are brought into the Main Memory (Swap In). Now the need arises to distinguish the pages which are in the RAM and which are not in the RAM. For the said purpose we use a valid/invalid bit, which indicates the presence of a page in memory or on disk. A valid/invalid bit is set to valid, when the page is legal and is in the memory (RAM). It is set to invalid in 2 situations:

(1) It is not valid or illegal, means that it does not lie in the logical address space of the process.

(2) Is valid, but is currently present on disk

The page table therefore now contains the frame number and the valid/invalid bit for each page. Whenever the page is brought into the RAM, it is set to valid bit and its frame number is allocated. The page table entry for a page that is not brought in RAM is marked as invalid.

This can be depicted as below:

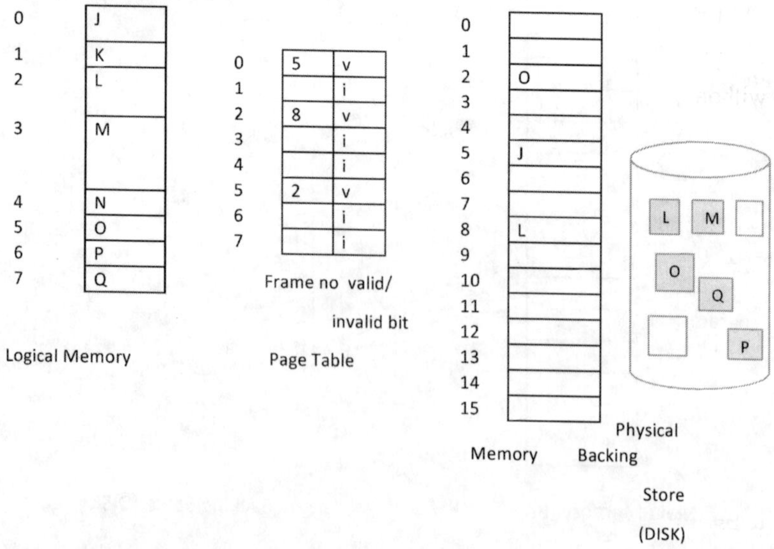

If the pager brings in the pages that were required by the process, then the process can execute normally. If a process requires a page that was not brought into the memory and that page is accessed, then it will cause a page fault. It can be seen by the h/w that the entry of that particular page in the page table is set to invalid bit. This causes a trap in the operating system. This trap has occurred because we tried to access a page which was not present in the RAM. Here is a list of steps that we have to follow if a page fault occurs:

(1) The first step is to check with an internal table that the access to the page was for a valid memory access or an invalid memory access. If it was an invalid memory access which means it tries to access beyond the logical address space of the process, then the process is terminated.

(2) If the attempt was to access a valid logical address space of that process and the page is not present in the RAM, then it continues and brings that page into the RAM.

(3) The next step is to find a free available frame in which the page can be brought in from the disk.

(4) To bring in the desired page, the disk performs a read operation on that page and puts it in the allocated frame.

(5) On completion of the read operation by the disk it modifies the internal table of the process to indicate that the page is in RAM or in other words it sets the valid/invalid bit to valid.

(6) Then the instruction can be restarted again.

Now it finds that the page is in the RAM, so it continues normally without causing a trap to the operating system.

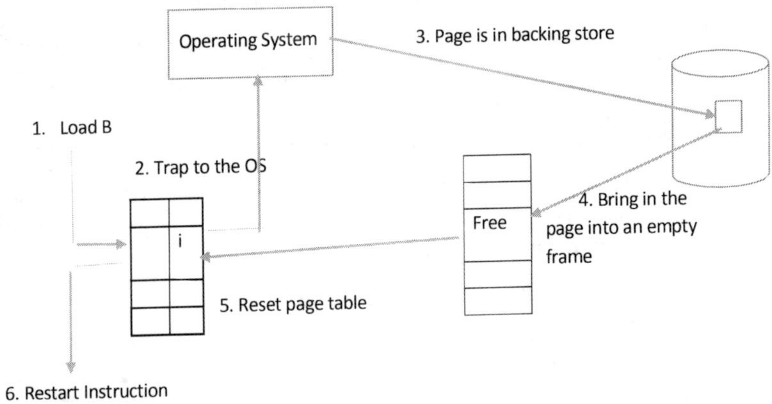

Performance of Demand Paging

The performance of a computer system can be affected greatly by the way how demand paging works. Here is a technique to compute the effective access time for a demand paged memory.

The memory access time = ma

= Ranges between 10 and 200 nanoseconds

If there are zero page faults then

Effective access time = memory access time

If the page faults are > 0 then

We need to read the desired page from disk into the RAM and then access the relevant word let us assume that the probability of a page fault is denoted by p, such that

$$0 <= p <= 1$$

The expectation of p would be considered to 0 when we are expecting that there are very less number of page faults.

The effective access time is computed as follows:

Effective access time = (1-p) * ma + p * page fault time

For the computation of effective access time, we would require a value of page fault service time.

The following sequence of events take place when a page fault occurs:

(1) Trap to Operating system.

(2) Save the user registers and process state.

(3) Find out that the interrupt was actually a page fault.

(4) Find out that it was a legal address lying in the logical address space of the process and if it was legal, then find the desired location of the page on disk.

(5) Bring a page from disk into a free frame:

   (a) Wait in the queue for this device until the read request is serviced

   (b) Wait till the device completes its seek time and latency time.

   (c) Transfer the page into the frame

(6) While waiting, you can allocate the CPU to another process which needs the CPU, in other words doing CPU scheduling.

(7) On completion of disk I/O, an interrupt will be raised.

(8) Save the contents of registers and the process state if we are executing step 6 i.e. CPU scheduling.

(9) Find out that the interrupt occurred from the Disk.

(10) Reset entries in the page table and other tables to indicate that the desired page is now in the memory.

(11) Wait for the time the CPU is allocated to the process.

(12) Get back the user registers, process state and the new page table and restart the interrupted instruction.

The above is a complete list of steps for a page fault. In many cases, all of the steps need not be executed. Some can be eliminated, such as step 6 is not executed. So the page fault service time can be categorised in 3 broad steps

(a) Service the page fault interrupt

(b) Read in the page

(c) Restart the process

The 1st and 3rd steps can be reduced to several hundred instructions by doing proper coding. They may vary from 1 to 100 microseconds each. The page switch time, will be nearly close to 8 milliseconds. A typical hard disk will have :

(1) Average latency time of 3 milliseconds (latency time is the time needed to bring the required sector under the read/write head)

(2) Seek time of 5 milliseconds

(3) Transfer time of 0.05 milliseconds

Paging time = 8 milliseconds

If the page fault service time is suppose 8 milliseconds and memory access time is 200 nanoseconds, then

Effective Access Time = (1-p) * 200 + p * 8 ms

= (1-p) * 200 + p * 8000000 (conversion to nanoseconds)

= 200 + 7999800*p

This shows that the effective access time is directly proportional to the page fault rate.

Let us take an example to understand the concept better

Consider a demand paged system, page table are held in registers. It takes 8 milliseconds to service a page fault, if an empty page(frame) is available or the replaced page is not modified and 20 milliseconds if the replaced page is modified. Memory access time (ma) is 100 nanoseconds. Assume that the page to be replaced is modified 70 percent of the time. What is the maximum acceptable page fault rate for an effective access time of no more than 200 nanoseconds.

Formula :

Effective access time $> (1\text{-}p) * ma + p *$ page fault service time

Where p is page fault rate

and ma is memory access time

Given :

Effective memory access time = 200 nanoseconds

ma (memory access time) = 100 nanoseconds

page fault service time = 8 ms (if not modified)

page fault service time = 20 ms (if modified)

We need to find the value of p, which is page fault rate

Now 70% of the time page is modified

And 30% of the time page is not modified

So putting all values together:

$= 200\text{ ns} > (1\text{-}p) * 100\text{ ns} + (70/100)*p * 20\text{ ms} + (30/100) * p * 8\text{ ms}$

Converting all to nanoseconds

$= 200 > 100 - 100*p + 14000000\, p + 2400000 * p$

$= 100 > 16400000 * p - 100 * p$

$= 100 > 16399900* p$

$= 100 / 16399900 > p$

$= 1/ 163999 > p$

$= 0.000006097\text{ ns} > p$

So the page fault rate should be kept less than these many nanoseconds.

6.10 Page Replacement

Following approach is taken for page replacement. If there is no free frame available in the physical memory, we make it free.

A page is made free by writing its contents to the swap space and updating the page table (and other tables) indicating that the page is no longer used in the physical memory.

The frame that just got free, is used to hold the contents of the page that just had been requested or faulted.

The page fault service which is modified is explained below:

(1) Find the desired page and its location on the disk.

(2) Find a free frame

  (a) If there is a frame which is free, then we use it

  (b) If no frame is free at the moment, use a page replacement algorithm to find a victim frame.

  (c) Write the victim frame to the disk, change the entries in page table and frame table accordingly.

(3) Bring in the desired page into the recently freed frame, change the entries in page and frame tables.

(4) Restart the user process.

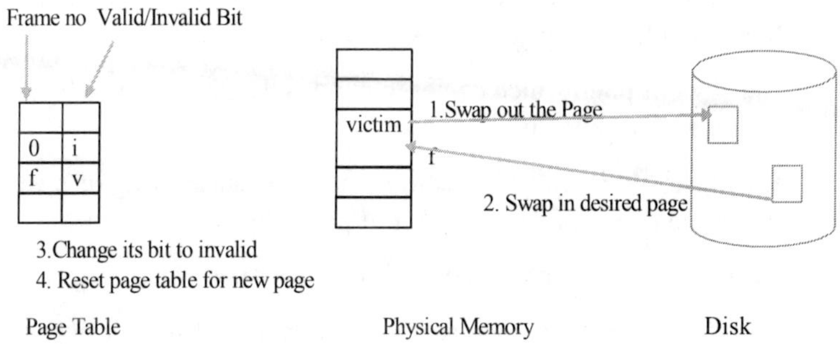

In case no frame is free, the transfer for a page requires 2 operations. One is to write the frame to the disk (Swap Out) and the other is to write the page from disk to the frame (Swap In).

In this case the overhead of page fault is double and correspondingly the effective access time is increased. This overhead can be reduced by making use of another bit called the modify bit or the dirty bit.

The above scenario requires that each page or frame has a modify bit associated with it in the h/w. The modify bit of a page will be set by the h/w if there has been any updation in the page, either any word or byte has been written onto it.

Whenever there is a requirement for a page to be swapped out, the modify bit is checked. If it is set, then the page has to be swapped out on to disk, and if it is not set, that means no modification has taken place on that page, then it need not be swapped out, since the page is already present on the disk.

This method can be helpful in read only pages also. Since read only pages can never be modified.

This scheme considerably reduces the time of page fault, since the I/O time is reduced by half. In demand paging and page replacement, enough of virtual memory is given to a process.

Two problems need to be solved in this case:

(1) Frame Allocation Algorithm

(2) Page Replacement Algorithm

The frame allocation algorithm decides how many frames need to be allocated to each process. The page-replacement algorithm decides which all frames need to be replaced.

There are a number of page replacement algorithms, we need to decide which one should we apply.

The obvious point which comes to mind is that the one which has the least number of page faults.

The algorithm is tested by running on a particular string of memory references and computing the number of page faults.

The string of memory references is called a reference string.

Now suppose we have the following reference string for evaluating the page replacement algorithm:

8, 2, 3, 4, 2, 5, 2, 6, 4, 5, 2, 5, 4, 3, 4, 2, 3, 8, 2, 3

Let us assume that our memory has 3 frames. Let us now discuss the 3 important page replacement algorithms.

(1) FIFO Page Replacement (First In First Out)

(2) Optimal Page Replacement

(3) LRU Page Replacement (Least Recently Used)

6.10.1 First In First Out Page Replacement

This is the most trivial algorithm.

Here for each page, a time is given when it is brought into memory. Whenever a page needs to be replaced, the one which is the oldest is removed. Here time is not recorded, a FIFO queue is maintained to hold the pages. To delete a page we choose the one which is at the head of the queue.

A page which has just been brought into memory is placed at the tail of the queue. Let us calculate how will the reference string work with a 3 frames of memory.

At the beginning when no page has been brought in till now, the 3 frames are empty.

The first three references (8, 2, 3), cause 3 page faults and their contents are placed in the 3 empty frames.

Next reference is of page 4, which replaces page 8 because page 8 was brought in first. Next reference in the string is of page 2, because 2 is already in the frame, so no page fault occurs. Then the next page in reference string is of page 5. Page 5 is asked for the first time, so it is not in memory and the oldest page to remove is now page 2. The next in string is reference to page 2, 2 has just been removed. So page 2 is no more in the 3 frames of the memory so it needs to be brought in again. This time it will remove page 3.

Here we pictorially depict the above string with FIFO algorithm used with 3 frames of memory.

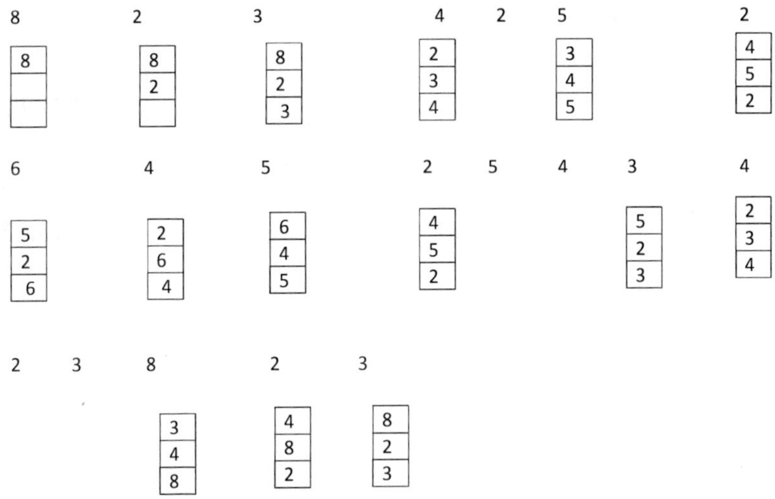

The above is a pictorial representation of the page faults. When a page fault occurs, a table representing 3 frames is shown with the contents in it. Whenever a page is demanded and it already exists in the 3 frames of memory, it is shown without the table and it further indicates that a page fault did not occur because it was already there. Now the number of page faults occurred have been shown by the tabular representation. We count that the number of tables above are 15, therefore it indicates that a total of 15 page faults have occurred.

The FIFO page replacement algorithm is easily implemented and easily understood. However, its performance may not be upto the mark all the time. Consider the following reference string

4, 5, 6, 7, 4, 5, 8, 4, 5, 6, 7, 8

The above figure shows how the number of page faults vary by increasing the number of frames. It is worth noting that for 4 frames the number of page faults is 10 and for 3 frames the number of page faults is 9. By increasing the number of frames, we expect that the number of page faults will reduce. But here increasing the number of frames, the number of page faults have also increased. This unusual phenomena is known as Belady's Anomaly. The page fault rate has increased as the number of allocated frames also increased. This is quite surprising because in general we expect that the performance of a process would increase by giving more memory to a process.

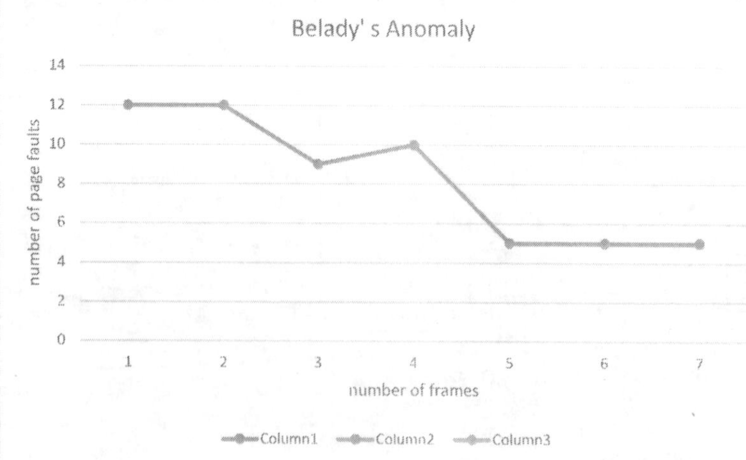

6.10.2 Optimal Page Replacement Algorithm

We see that Belady's Anomaly does not perform as expected. So the optimal page replacement was discovered. The algorithm does not suffer from Belady's Anomaly and has the lowest rate of page faults. It states "Replace the page that will not be used for the longest period of time". This algorithm ensures that the least number of page faults will occur for a fixed number of frames. Consider the same reference string used for the FIFO algorithm.

8, 2, 3, 4, 2, 5, 2, 6, 4, 5, 2, 5, 4, 3, 4, 2, 3, 8, 2, 3

The optimal page replacement algorithm gives us 9 page faults. Since the 3 frame memory is empty initially, so the string (8, 2, 3) yields 3 page faults and fills in the memory. The reference to page 4 replaces page 8, because page 8 will be used at the last (18th reference), considering the references to string (8, 2, 3). Here page 2 will be required at 5th reference and page 3 will be required at 14th reference. So the farthest element from here is page 8. Next in memory after 8, 2, 3, 4 is page 2. Page 2 is already in memory, so it does not result into a page fault. The next reference is to page 5. Out of (2, 3, 4) page 3 will be required furthest from here. So it causes a page faults and removes page 3. The 3 frames of memory are now (2, 5, 4).

Let us pictorially show how the page faults appear for the reference string.

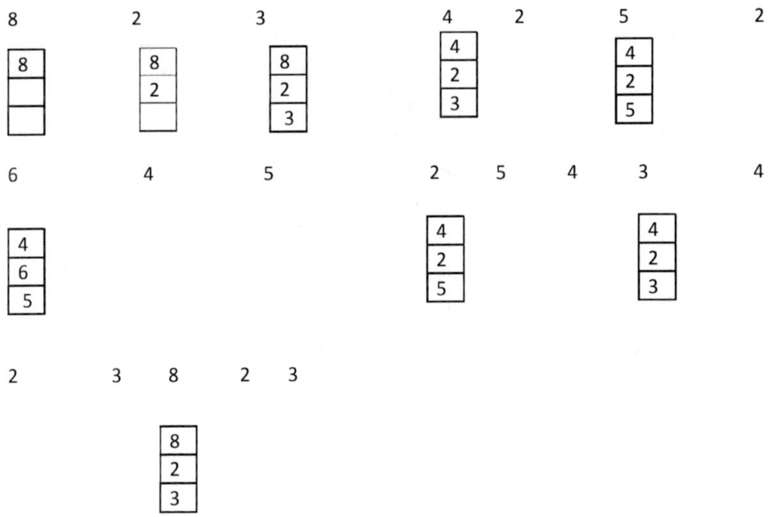

So we can see that 9 page faults have occurred. The OPT algorithm is good for theoretical purposes, but in actual implementation it is not really possible, since we are required to see the future that which page is furthest. This is not possible in real life because while computing the algorithm, we cannot determine which pages will be close and which page will be far from current position.

As a result, the optimal algorithm is used mainly for comparing the performance of algorithms.

6.10.2 Least Recently Used Algorithm (LRU)

To counter the above problem of requiring the future knowledge of the reference string, we consider an algorithm which does not require seeing in the future and its performance is also better than FIFO. The algorithm is based on the fact that most of the time the computer executes the same instruction again and again. Suppose a for loop executes 30 times, then the same instruction of the for loop would be required again and again. So the pages which was most recently would be required in the near future.

So here we replace a page that has not been used for the longest period of time. The approach is the least recently used algorithm. Let us demonstrate with the help of our reference string used in both of the above algorithms.

8, 2, 3, 4, 2, 5, 2, 6, 4, 5, 2, 5, 4, 3, 4, 2, 3, 8, 2, 3

Initially the 3 frame memory is empty so the first 3 pages result in 3 page faults. When the reference to page 4 occurs, LRU sees the most recently used pages are 2 and 3, so it replaces page 8. So now our 3 memory frame has (2,3,4). Next page reference is to page 5. Page 5 sees the most recently used are page 2 and page 4, therefore it replaces page 3. Next page reference is to page 2, this is already in the 3 frame memory, so we need not replace it. Then comes reference to page 6, so out of (5,2,4), the most recently used are (2, 5), so it removes page 4, without taking into consideration that page 4 is required just after that.

So here we pictorially see that 12 page faults have occurred, which is better than FIFO and lesser than OPT. But still the best choice is LRU since OPT cannot be implemented.

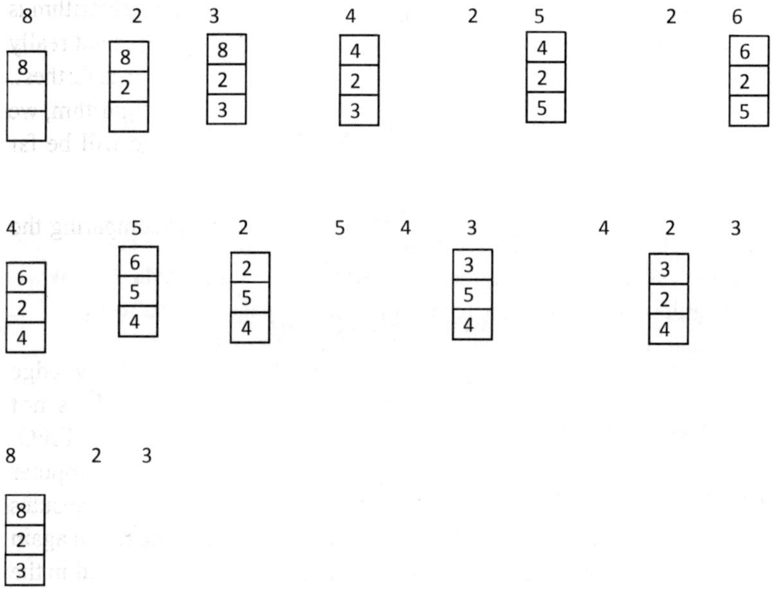

How can we implement LRU

As you can see LRU algorithm needs some kind of a timer to track which is the least recently used page and which is most recently used. The implementation is possible in 2 prominent ways:

(1) To use a counter

(2) To use a stack

In case of a counter, each page table entry has an associated time-of-use field and a logical clock. The clock gets incremented whenever a reference to a page is made. At the increment of the clock the contents of clock register are copied to the time-of-use field in the page table. In this way the time of lest reference is made available to us. The page with the smallest value is replaced.

The disadvantage with this method is that we need to search the entire page table to find which is the LRU page and also there is an overhead of copying the contents of the clock register to the time-of-use field whenever a memory access takes place.

In case of a stack, the stack of page numbers is kept. Whenever a reference to a page is made, it is removed and put on top of the stack. By this method, the page which is most recently used is available on top of the stack. The page which is least recently used is put at the bottom of the stack.

Both OPT and LRU are free from Belady's Anamoly.

6.11. Thrashing

Page fault occurs when sufficient number of frames are not available to a process. If the desired number of frames is not available, then it will page fault again and again trying to bring in pages which are required immediately. This high rate of paging is known as thrashing.

The formal definition of thrashing is that it spends more time doing paging than executing.

6.11.1 What is the cause of Thrashing

Thrashing causes degradation in performance of the system. It happens as a chain of events which are described below:

At first the operating system monitors the CPU utilisation. If the utilisation of CPU is less, the OS brings in a new program into the RAM trying to increase the degree of multiprogramming so that CPU utilisation can be improved.

After that, the OS again starts monitoring CPU utilisation. Now the scenario is that the new process requires some frames for its execution. So it page faults. So in doing that it removes the pages that it doesn't need, but they are required by the previous process. So there is more swapping done in and out. These processes start waiting in the device queue for I/O and leave the ready queue of the CPU. This further deteriorates the CPU utilisation. On seeing this, the OS tries to increase the degree of multiprogramming even further. Now the number of empty frames are required even more, which results in more paging. In this case, we say that thrashing has occurred. And page faults start occurring at a very high rate.

As a result, the effective memory access time is also increased. The throughput is very less, because no time is spent in doing any useful work, only in and out of pages is taking place.

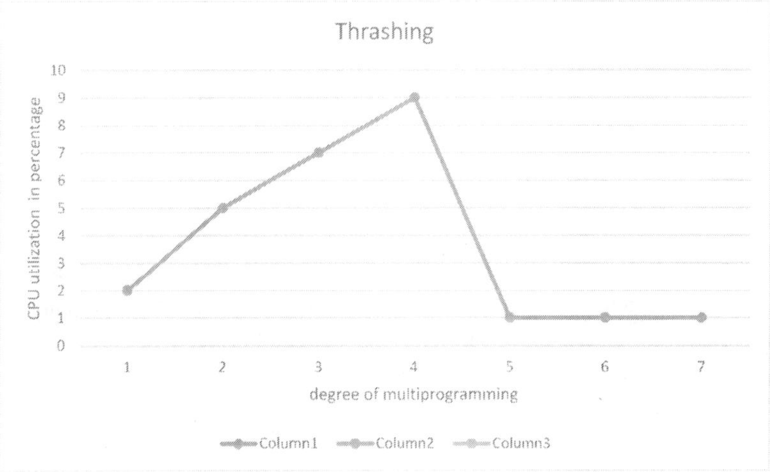

6.11.2 How to Prevent Thrashing

A process should be provided with that many frames that it requires. The question arises as to how to find out that a process requires how many frames. There are a number of techniques to find out.

A working set model is one of the ways. This model finds how many frames a process is actually using. This model explains about the locality model of program execution. The locality model states that as the process progresses in its execution, it starts moving from one locality to another locality.

A locality is a set of pages that are used together actively. A program is made up of several different localities which may overlap. For example, a function in a program defines a locality. In a function there are references made to the instructions of the function call, its local and global variables are also referenced. When the function is exited, that locality is left. A program defines its localities based on the structure of the program and its data structures. Locality model is also used in caching. Suppose a program enters one of its localities, to get the locality the process will page fault. Once all the instructions of the locality are made available, then there will be no need to page fault more.

Now it will page fault only when the program changes its locality. If the number of frames required by the current locality is not made available to the process, then it will thrash because it is unable to keep all pages required by its locality in memory.

Working Set Model

Working set model is based on the concept of locality. A Δ(delta) defines a window of the working set. This window is used to examine the most recent pages which lie into it. The set of pages in the most recent page reference is the working set. If a page is currently active, then it will be present in the working set. If the page becomes inactive, then it automatically drops out from the working set Δ(delta) time units after its last reference.

This working set defines an approximation of the program locality. For example, given below is a sequence of memory references shown for a process.

4,8,3,7,9,9,9,9,7,3,8,4,5,6,3,4,5,6,6,6,5,6,5,6,6,6,3,5,4,5,6,6,6,5,6,6.6.....

Δ(delta) Δ(delta)

ws (t1) = {3,4,7,8,9}

ws(t2) = {5,6}

if the working set window is Δ(delta) = 10 memory references,

then the working set at time t1 = {3,4,7,8,9}

and working set changes at time t2 = {5,6}

Caching

The CPU fetches instructions from RAM after they are made available from the disk. As and when the memory is referenced (RAM), it is stored in yet another faster storage known as cache. When memory is referenced again, the CPU finds out whether cache is having it before asking from RAM. If the information is available in cache, it will not go to RAM. If it is not present in cache, we will extract from RAM and put in the cache also at the same time under the assumption that we will soon require it again. The size of the cache is limited, very much smaller than the RAM. The performance of cache can be improved by selecting the right size of cache and the replacement policy.

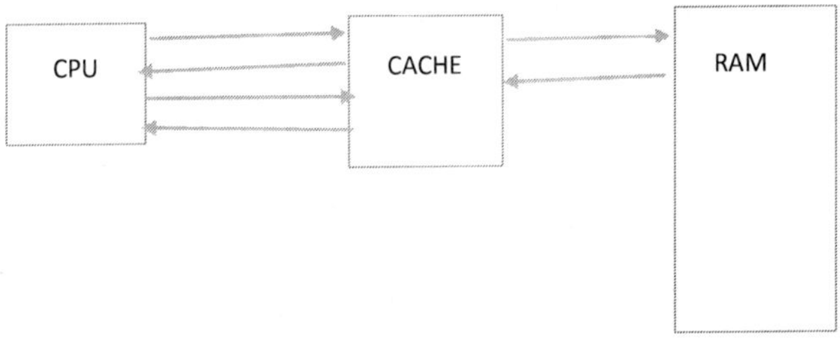

Solution to selected problems

Q1. Consider a logical address space of eight pages of 1024 words, each mapped unto a physical memory of 32 frames then:

(a) How many bits in the logical address

(b) How many bits in the physical address

Ans.

Logical address

P	d

Physical Address

f	d

(a) Bits in Logical Address:

Logical address space size = 2^m

Page Size = 2^n

Page no p	Offset d
m-n bits	n bits

Here Page Size =1024 * 4 bytes (since word size = 4)

$= 2^{10} * 2^2$

$= 2^{12}$

$= 2^n$

= Therefore, n = 12

Logical address space is $2^m = 8$ * page size

$= 8 * 2^{12}$

$= 2^3 * 2^{12}$

$= 2^{15}$

Therefore, 15 bits in logical address space with an offset (d) of 12 bits.

(b) Physical Address space = f + d

= 32 frames + offset d

= $2^5 + 2^{12}$

= 2^{17}

Therefore, 17 bits in physical address space.

Q2. Consider a demand paged system. Page tables are stored in main memory which has an access time of 100 nanoseconds. The TLB can hold 8 page table entries and has an access time of 10 nanoseconds. During the execution of a process, it is found that 80% of the time, a required page table entry exists in TLB and only 2% of the references cause page faults. The average time to service page faults is 2 milliseconds. Compute the effective memory access time.

Ans.

Effective memory access time = (1-p)*ma X p X page fault service time.

Here 80% of the time = TLB access

2% of the time = page fault occurs

Therefore, 18 % of the time = is page table accessed

Therefore, (1-p) *ma = TLB access + page table access

P X page fault service time = page faults and the time it takes to service.

TLB access time = 80/100 * 10 nanoseconds

= 8 nanoseconds

Page table access time = 18/100 * 100 nanoseconds

= 18 nanoseconds

Page fault = 2/100 * 2000000 nanoseconds

= 40000 nanoseconds

Therefore, effective memory access time = 8 + 18 + 40000 nanoseconds

= 40026 nanoseconds

Chapter - 7

Input Output Management

7.1 Input Output Devices

Let us see what type of I/O Devices are available to us. They can be categorised as follows:

(1) Character-Stream or Block

A character stream device transfers each byte one after another. A block device transfers a block of bytes as a whole unit.

(2) Sequential or Random Access

A sequential device transfers data in a particular order which is determined by the device. A random access method is used to find data at any random location on the disk.

(3) Synchronous or Asynchronous

In a synchronous mode, the data transfers from a device takes place in predictable response time. In an asynchronous mode, the data transfers from a device takes place in an irregular or unpredictable response time.

(4) Sharable or Dedicated

A dedicated device only takes care of a single process. Whereas a sharable device can cater to a number of processes concurrently.

(5) Speedy or Non-Speedy Devices

Slow devices run at a speed of few bytes per second and speedy devices run upto a few gigabytes per second.

(6) Read Only, Write Only and Read/Write Devices

Some devices perform read only operation other devices perform write only operation and yet another type of devices perform both read and write operation.

Block and Character Devices

The interface of block devices is pretty much able to capture all the features relating to accessing disk drives. These devices are able to perform read() and write() operations. In case of random access, they can also perform the seek() operation. The character device nature is best described by taking the example of a keyboard. It has a character stream interface, this has a linear stream of bytes. The functions that it can perform are put() and get(), which work on a single character.

Network Devices

Network devices differ significantly in performance and addressing characteristics when compared to disk I/O. A network I/O interface is provided with every operating system which is quite different from the disk I/O. Disk I/O performs standard read(), write() and seek() operations. In UNIX and Windows NT, there exists a network interface known as the network socket interface. The operating system issues system calls to create a socket. A socket is created in every application which wants to communicate over the network. A socket created in a local application connect to a socket created in a remote application. The local socket keeps listening at its end, and when a request for connection comes from the remote application, both sockets connect and send and receive packets over the transmission.

A socket is made up of an IP address and a port number. The IP address is the address of the machine on the www and the port number is of the port on which the process is running.

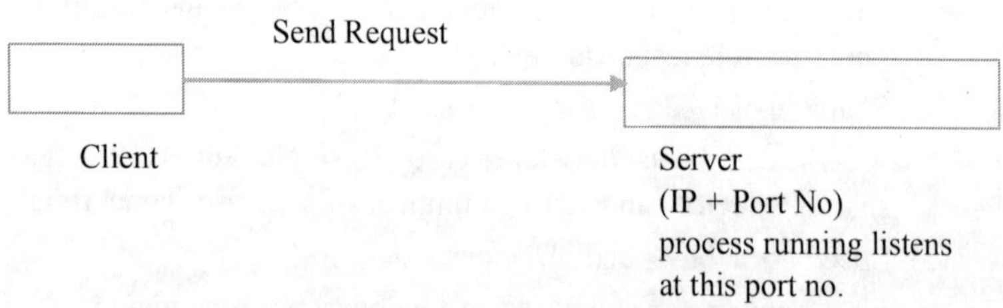

Both client and server use sockets to pass message to each other. User Datagram Protocol (UDP) and Transmission Control Protocol (TCP) both use sockets to pass information.

Clocks and Timers

Each computer system is equipped with a clock and timer. They perform the following tasks:

(1) Give the current time

(2) Give the elapsed time

(3) Set a timer to trigger an operation p at time

There is a hardware called the programmable interval timer, which is responsible for measuring elapsed time and triggering operations. The programmable interval timer is set to a particular value, for which it waits and then raises an interrupt. This can be set to a particular value for interrupting periodically or to interrupt only once.

You may recall that in round robin scheduling algorithm, a time slice was used. So this interrupt was set periodically to pre-empt a process after its time slice was over. Also it can be used to reduce network congestion by removing processes which are proceeding too slow.

Blocking and Non-Blocking I/O

System call interface is equipped to chose between either a Blocking I/O or a Non-Blocking I/O. A blocking I/O can be chosen by an application and for that a blocking system call is initiated. On receiving an I/O system call, the process is suspended and moved from the CPU's run queue to an I/O waiting queue. After the I/O operation is complete, the process gets back in the run queue where it is allowed to resume execution. On resuming the execution, the process is given all the values that the system call had returned. These system calls are asynchronous in nature, i.e. the time taken by them to execute is varying in nature or unpredictable.

On the other hand, some operating systems use blocking system calls in their interface. Code of blocking applications is easier to understand than that of non-blocking counterpart. In some applications, it is required to issue non-blocking I/O. The example of non-blocking I/O is while dealing with a keyboard input or mouse input, which are processing the data and displaying the data on the screen. Another example that comes to mind is video application that take their input from a file present on the disk and transfer to the frames of RAM. Also it is simultaneously decompressing the data and displaying the images on the monitor. I/O applications can be overlapped using multithreaded applications. In this case we say that threads are performing blocking system calls while others are simply continuing their execution.

Kernel I/O Subsystems

The Kernel is responsible for providing I/O related services such as:

(1) Scheduling

(2) Buffering

(3) Caching

(4) Spooling

(5) Device Reservation

(6) Error Handling

These are performed by the Kernel's I/O subsystem, and they are built on the hardware and device driver infrastructure. The I/O subsystem has to take care of itself by preventing itself from errant processes and malicious users.

7.2 Input/Output Scheduling

We need to find an order in which the applications will be executed and this is known as I/O scheduling. Applications execute system calls in a particular order that order is generally not the best order to do I/O scheduling. The overall performance of a system can greatly be improved by proper scheduling. The device can be shared among processes in a fair manner so that it can reduce the average waiting time for an I/O to complete. Let us demonstrate with the help of an example.

Suppose a disk arm is placed near the beginning of the disk and there are 3 applications, namely A, B, and C which issue a blocking read calls to the disk. Suppose Application A wants to access the end part of the disk. Application B wants to access the beginning part of the disk and application C wants to access at the middle of the disk. The order is displayed below:

Application A	Application B	Application C
End	Beginning	Middle

The distance travelled by the disk's arm can be greatly reduced if the applications move in the following order:

Application B, Application C, Application A

Scheduling is done by the operating system by having a wait queue for each device containing requests. Whenever a blocking I/O system call is generated by an application, its request is put on the device's queue.

The order of the queue may be rearranged by the scheduler so that overall efficiency of the system is maintained and the average response time is much better for applications.

It also tries to be fair by ensuring that every process receives the service properly. It also takes care when priority based scheduling is done.

In case the kernel has asynchronous I/O, then it needs to take care of the fact that the number of I/O requests would be coming in at the same time. In that case, the OS attaches the wait queue of each device into device status table. The table is managed by the Kernel and it has one entry each for an I/O device.

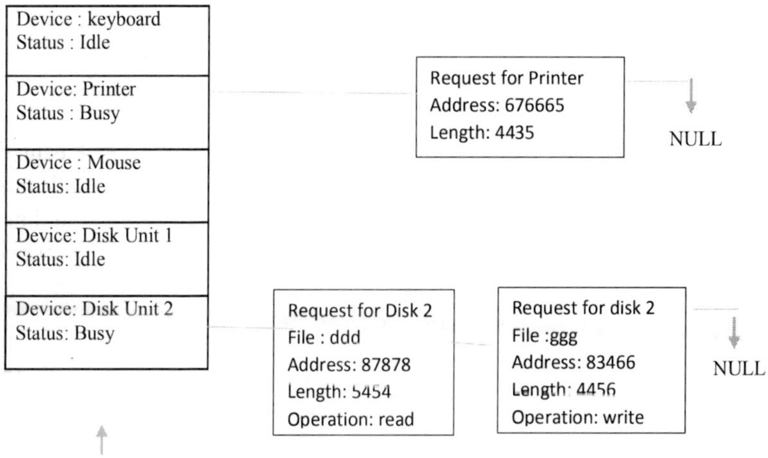

Device Status table

Each entry of the table contains the information about each device. It has parameters such as status, name, operation, address, length. If the device is catering to some process, its status will be busy and other parameters will be populated.

The OS uses an I/O Subsystem to improve the computer's efficiency in scheduling I/O operations.

The other storage space methods that are used by the OS to improve efficiency are:

(1) Buffering

(2) Caching

(3) Spooling

Buffering

Transferring of data takes place between two devices or between a device and an application. Buffer is a memory area which helps in doing so. Buffering is done because the speed of 2 devices is different. A producer may produce give more data than the consumer can use it.

Eg is modem and disk

Disk is thousands times faster than a modem. A buffer is created in main memory so that it can store the bytes which modem sends. When the whole buffer is full, then it can be written on the disk in a single operation. The disk does not do its write operation instantaneously. So to store the changes, an area of memory is required. With disk and modem, 2 buffers are required. When the modem fills the first buffer, the disk is requested for a write() operation, in that time, the modem uses the 2nd buffer to fill itself while first buffer is being written on disk. When the first buffer has written to disk, then it starts to fill it up again till the time 2nd buffer is writing to disk.

Another area where buffering is used is in the area of computer networks. The sender fragments the data into packets and sends them. The receiver accumulates all packets. The packets do not arrive in the order in which they were sent. So a buffer is used in the receiver's side to assemble them in order.

Caching

Cache is a fast memory area that has copies of data from the RAM. Accessing data from the cache is much efficient than getting it from RAM. Whereas buffer has data which is given to it for further processing. Caching and buffering both have different functions, but at times they may be required to work together. They are expected to work together in copy semantics.

Copy Semantics

Suppose there is an application which is interested in writing a buffer of data to the disk. It will call the write() system call, by telling from where in buffer to write and how many bytes to write. Suppose after the system call returns changes have been done in the application's content.

With the help of copy semantics, we will be able to have that version of data written to the disk as the one which was there at the time the application issued the system call. There will not be any further changes done to the application buffer.

A simple way in which operating system guarantees copy semantics is that write() system call copies the application's data into the kernel buffer before finishing its work and returning control to the application. Now the changes will be taken from the kernel buffer, so that the changes made in the application's buffer do not have any effect.

In OS when copy semantics is done, then disk I/O is scheduled to work efficiently. Buffers in the main memory are used to hold disk data. The buffers here are also used as cache, so that I/O efficiency of files is improved in application for reading and writing. When an I/O request for a file is received by kernel, the kernel first checks to see if that is present in the buffer's cache or not. If it is there, then the region of memory can be copied directly from buffer instead of invoking a disk I/O.

Also when disk is written, the buffer cache holds all the accumulated data that needs to be written on disk.

Spooling

A spool is a buffer which is used to hold output for a device. A typical example of this is the printer. Spool stands for Simultaneous Peripheral Operations On Line. The printer is used to serve one job at one time. There may be a number of applications that need to print without their data being interleaved. Spooling helps in putting all the jobs which need to be printed in a proper queue. The printer can then pick up from there and print them.

7.3 Disk Scheduling

We need to schedule disk access so that performance becomes efficient. We need to ensure that the access time is quick and the bandwidth of the disk is large enough. The access time is measured by two major components:

(1) The Seek Time

(2) Rotational Latency

Seek Time

This is the time required for the disk arm to make its head point to the cylinder containing the required sector.

Rotational Latency

After pointing to the correct cylinder in seek time. This additional time is required to bring the correct sector under the head of the disk by rotating it.

Disk Bandwidth

Another criteria for measuring performance is disk bandwidth, which is calculated as follows:

The total number of bytes transferred divided by the difference between the time taken to issue the first request and the time at which the last transfer was serviced.

By proper ordering of I/O requests being serviced, we can improve our accessing time and the bandwidth. A system call is initiated by the operating system whenever a process need to read something from the disk or write something to the disk.

Each request provides the following information:

(1) Whether the operation is read or write
(2) The disk address where the transfer is to be made
(3) The memory address where the transfer is to be made
(4) How many number of sectors need to be transferred

The requests may be serviced immediately if the required disk drive and controller are available right now. In case our disk drive or controller are not available, i.e. they are busy servicing some other request, then our request will be placed in the queue where all the pending requests are waiting.

In case we have a multiprogrammed environment, where a number of processes are trying to access the disk, then there will be multiple requests lined up. On the completion of one request, the OS has to decide which one should be serviced next. How does OS make a choice is a question to be answered.

There are a number of scheduling algorithms such as:

(1) FCFS (First Come First Serve) Scheduling
(2) SSTF (Shortest Seek Time First) Scheduling
(3) SCAN Scheduling
(4) C-SCAN Scheduling

(5) LOOK Scheduling

(6) C-LOOK Scheduling

7.3.1 First Come First Serve Scheduling

FCFS is the simplest form of disk scheduling algorithm. This is a fair algorithm but it is not able to provide the quickest service. The cylinder that comes first is the one which is accessed first.

Let us take an example to explain it. Suppose we have the following cylinders to be accessed in the given order:

86, 171, 25, 110, 2, 112, 53, 55

Suppose our disk head is positioned initially at the cylinder 41.

Then our algorithm will move from 41 to 86, from 86 to 171, from 171 to 25 and so on. Let us denote it pictorially:

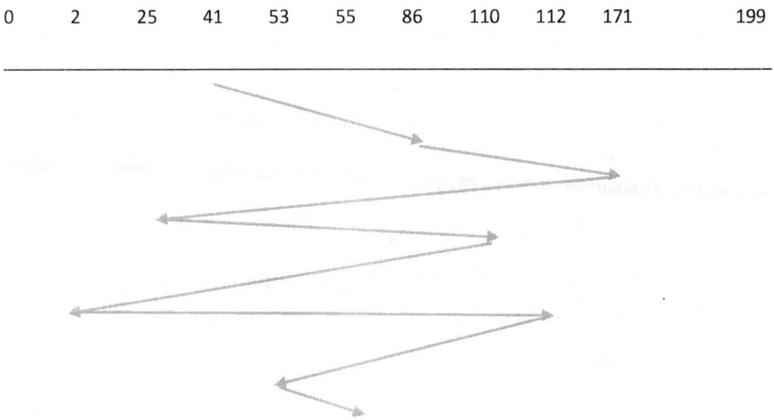

The calculations of head movement are as follows, they will be positive numbers because it is calculating the movement of the head, the distance between 2 cylinders.

41 – 86 = 45

86 – 171 = 85

171 – 25 = 146

25 – 110 = 85

110 – 2 = 108

2 – 112 = 110

112 – 53 = 59

53 – 55 = 2

Total = 45 + 85 + 146 + 85 + 108 + 110 + 59 + 2

= 640 cylinders to be moved

The drawback of this algorithm is that the head movements are going from one end to another end, just because they arrived in that order. So there are wide swings from here to there. If we use some method intelligently. Then these wide swings can be addressed and our performance can also be improved.

7.3.2 Shortest Seek Time First Scheduling

This algorithm tries to service the request which are lying close to each other from the current head position. Instead of moving far distances away from one another. This algorithm assumes that the shortest distance away is where the pointer will go.

The algorithm selects the request which has the least seek time from the position it is at right now.

Let us take an example to understand it. We are taking the same sequence of cylinders that we used with FCFS algorithm. With our head initially at position 41

86, 171, 25, 110, 2, 112, 53, 55

Now from 41, it will either go to left or to right. To the left of 41 lies 25, and to the right of 41 lies 53.

41 – 25 = 16

41 – 53 = 12

So out of 16 and 12, 12 is shortest, so from 41 it will move to 53. Now it is currently placed at 53. So from 53, 55 is the shortest, so it will move to 55. Then from 55 either it will go to right where lies 86, or to the left where lies 25.

55 – 86 = 31

55 – 25 = 30

So out of 31 and 30, 30 is shortest, so it will move to 25. Let us see pictorially:

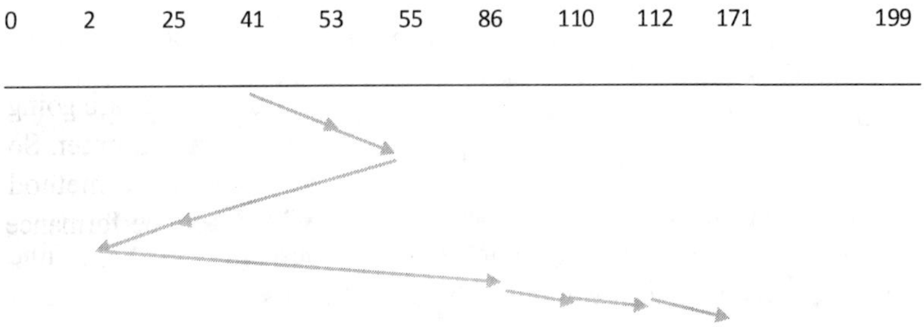

The total head movements are calculated as follows:

41 – 53 = 12

53 – 55 = 2

55 – 25 = 30

25 – 2 = 23

2 – 86 = 84

86 – 110 = 24

110 – 112 = 2

112 – 171 = 59

Total = 12 + 2 + 30 + 23 + 84 + 24 + 2 + 59

= 236

This results in a total cylinder movement of 236. SSTF is quite similar to SJF(Shortest Job First Scheduling) and it may lead to starvation as the cylinder requests may be coming in at any time.

Suppose I am near cylinder 2 and a request for cylinder 4 comes, then after 2 the scheduler was to go to cylinder 171, but because 4 is closer than 171, so it starts processing cylinder 4. After that is done, suppose now a request comes in for cylinder 6, so it will start processing 6 instead of 171. In this case the request for cylinder 171 is starved because it it not getting a chance to be serviced.

7.3.3 SCAN

In this algorithm, the disk arm starts at one end of the disk and moves towards the other end. It services requests as it encounters while moving in one direction until it reaches the end of the disk, then it will reverse its direction to go to the other end. In this way the head of the disk arm scans back and forth. Before the algorithm starts we need to know the direction in which the head is moving and also the initial position of the head.

Let us assume that the position of the head is at 41 and the direction of the head is towards 0. Then the head will service the request for cylinder 25 and then go to 2 and from 2 to 0. At 0 it will change direction and move to 53, from 53 to 55 and so on till it reaches 171.

If a request arrives a little ahead of the current request in the same direction, then that will be catered to. But if a request arrives a little behind the current request, then it will not be serviced. It will be taken care of when the head starts moving in the opposite direction.

Let us take the same reference string as above to demonstrate the working of the algorithm.

With our head initially at position 41, and moving in the direction towards cylinder 0.

86, 171, 25, 110, 2, 112, 53, 55

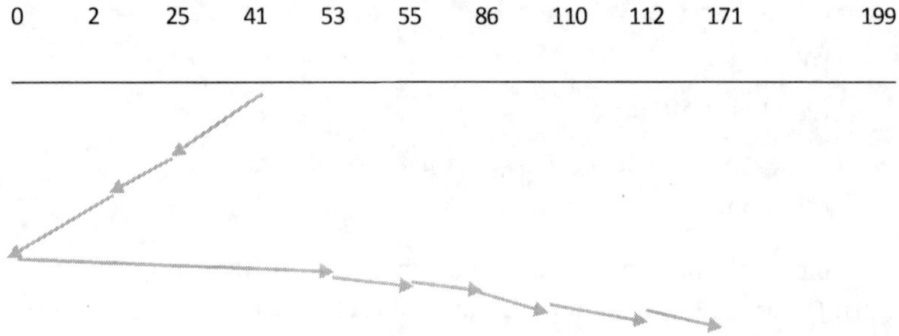

Total head movements:

41 – 25 = 16

25 – 2 = 23

2 – 0 = 2

0 – 53 = 53

53 – 55 = 2

55 – 86 = 31

86 – 110 = 24

110 – 112 = 2

112 – 171 = 59

Total = 16 + 23 + 2 + 53 + 2 + 31 + 24 + 2 + 59
= 212

This algorithm moves disk arm across the full width of the disk.

7.3.4 C- SCAN (Circular SCAN)

This is a variant of the SCAN algorithm known as Circular SCAN. This tries to provide a much uniform wait time. Just like SCAN, the C-SCAN moves its head from one end of disk to another along the way it services requests which are encountered. When the head reaches one end of the disk, then it immediately traverses to the other end of the disk without catering to any requests which it finds on its way. Then from that end it starts to move to the other servicing the requests which were left out and now need servicing.

Let us explain with the help of our example. Initial head position 41 and moving towards 199.

86, 171, 25, 110, 2, 112, 53, 55

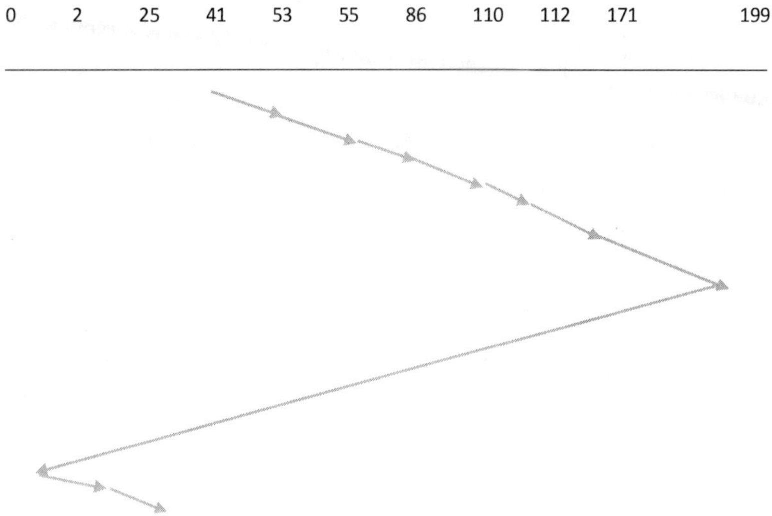

Counting the head movements, we get it as follows:

41 – 53 = 12

53 – 55 = 2

55 – 86 = 31

86 – 110 = 24

110 – 112 = 2

112 – 171 = 59

171 – 199 = 28

199 – 0 = 199

0 – 2 = 2

2 – 25 = 23

Total = 12 + 2 + 31 + 24 + 2 + 59 + 28 + 199 + 2 + 23

= 382

As we can see the number of head movements have increased.

7.3.5 LOOK Scheduling

The drawback with SCAN and C-SCAN is that they move from one end of the disk to another end taking one full width. This is not a good way to be implemented. Here the disk arm goes as far as there are request in one direction and need not go to the end of the disk. So here in this algorithm as soon as it services the last request at one end, then it will reverse the direction immediately without going to end of disk. And on reversing back it services all the requests which are encountered on the way till it reaches the last request in that particular direction.

Here it keeps looking for requests, that is why the name LOOK is given.

Let us take our example to explain. Initial head position 41 and moving towards 199.

86, 171, 25, 110, 2, 112, 53, 55

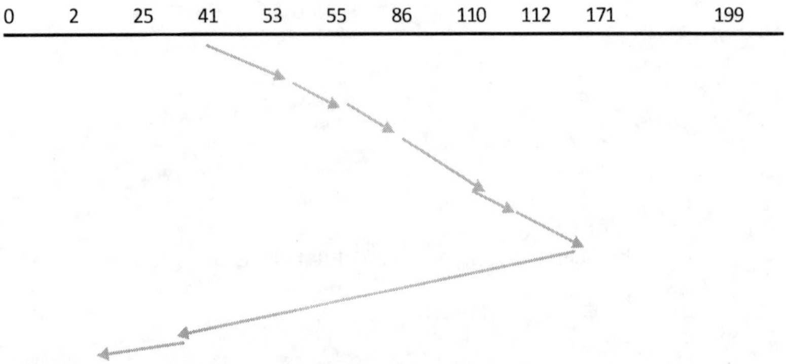

To calculate the number of head movements, we proceed as follows:

41 – 53 = 12

53 – 55 = 2

55 – 86 = 31

110 – 86 = 24

112 – 110 = 2

112 – 171 = 59

171 – 25 = 146

25 – 2 = 23

Total = 12 + 2 + 31 + 24 + 2 + 59 + 146 + 23

= 299

7.3.6 C-LOOK Scheduling

This combines the properties of LOOK and C-SCAN. First it considers that the disk is circular. It needs the direction of the head and the initial position of the head. It then moves in that direction catering to all the requests that it finds from there. It does not go to the end of the disk but reverses its direction. It does not service requests which it finds on the reverse way. It goes to the first request in the reverse direction and starts serving the requests which were left out.

Let us take our example to explain. Initial head position 41 and moving towards 199.

86, 171, 25, 110, 2, 112, 53, 55

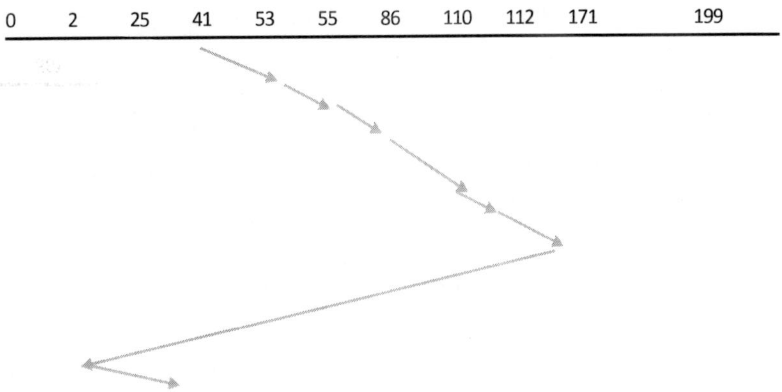

Total head movements are calculated as follows:

41 – 53 = 12

53 – 55 = 2

55 – 86 = 31

110 – 86 = 24

112 – 110 = 2

112 – 171 = 59

171 – 2 = 169

2 – 25 = 23

Total = 12 + 2 + 31 + 24 + 2 + 59 + 169 + 23

= 322

7.4 RAID Structure

If our disks are large in number, then they can afford to operate in parallel, thereby improving the rate at which data is written to disk. As the disks are many, so it provides us with the opportunity to have duplicate data which leads to reliability. If one disk fails, then other can take up its work so that data is not lost.

RAID is one of those disk organisation technique which offers better performance and better reliability. RAID stands for Redundant Array of Independent Disks. RAID is focused to provide reliability and performance rather than focusing on economy.

Improving Reliability Vs Redundancy

To provide reliability, we will need to have redundant data. In which case we will have to store extra information which is generally not required but would prove very helpful if any failure occurs and can help to recreate the data. In other words, disk failure will not result in loss of data.

The simplest way to achieve redundancy is to duplicate every disk. This is known as mirroring.

In mirroring every logical disk has 2 physical disks and write operation is performed on both of those disks. This is known as mirrored volume. If one of the disk fails, then data can be read from the other disk.

The loss of data will take place if the 2nd disk fails before the first failed disk could be populated with the data. In this case loss of data will take place.

The mean time to failure is because of two factors:

(1) The mean time to repair

(2) The mean time to failure of an independent disk.

Mean time to repair is the time taken to repair a failed disk and to get back the data on it.

If the failure of both disks are independent of one another, which means that the failure of one disk has not affected the failure of another disk, then

If men time of failure of one disk = 50,000 hours

And mean time to repair = 5 hours

The mean time to data loss of a mirrored disk system

$$= (50000)^2 / (2 * 5)$$

$$= 250 * 10^6$$

Improvement in Performance via Parallelism

Let us see how we can improve performance by parallelly accessing the disks. The disk mirroring technique helps in doubling the rate at which read requests are done. Read requests can be sent to either of the 2 disks. The transfer rate remains the same as a single disk but the number of read can be doubled per unit time. The transfer rate can also be improved if we have multiple disks. There is a simple technique called data stripping which splits the bits of each byte across multiple disks. This is known as bit level stripping. For example, if there is an array of 8 disks, then we can write bit i of each byte to disk i. The array of 8 disks may be considered as a single disk with sectors that are 8 times the normal size and their access rate is also 8 times the normal rate. In this technique every disk participates in each read or write. So the number of accesses processed per second remains the same as a single disk. But each access can fetch 8 times as many bytes as the time compared to a single disk. There is another technique called block level stripping, in which blocks are stripped across multiple disks. We can similarly perform byte level or sector level stripping.

We achieve parallelism in disk systems through the stripping technique.

RAID LEVELS

Mirroring ensures that reliability can be achieved but at an expensive cost. Stripping on the other hand can give us a higher transfer rate but improved reliability cannot be guaranteed.

There are other techniques which propose that redundancy will be there at low cost and disk stripping combined with a number of parity bits can give better results. These techniques have their own cost vs performance trade off and are designed as different RAID levels. They are discussed as follows:

p – indicates the error correcting bits

c – indicate a duplicate copy of the disk

four disk are necessary to store data and other extra disk will be used for storing redundant information which may be required at the time of failure recovery.

7.4.1 RAID LEVEL 0

Also known as non-redundant stripping. At this level the following is performed:

(1) Stripping done at block level

(2) There is no redundancy

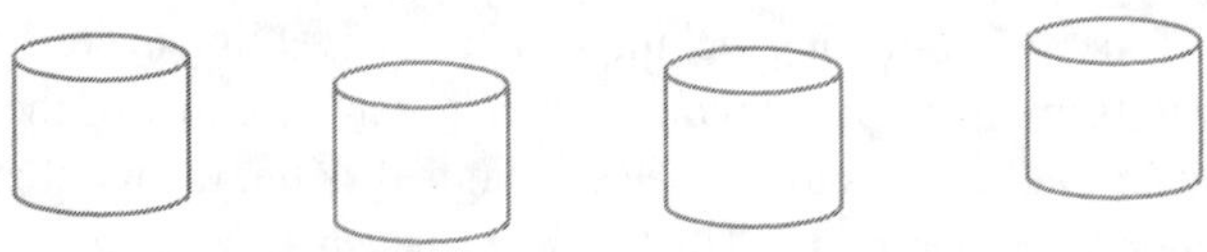

7.4.2 RAID LEVEL 1

Also known as disk mirroring. Here they are mirrored.

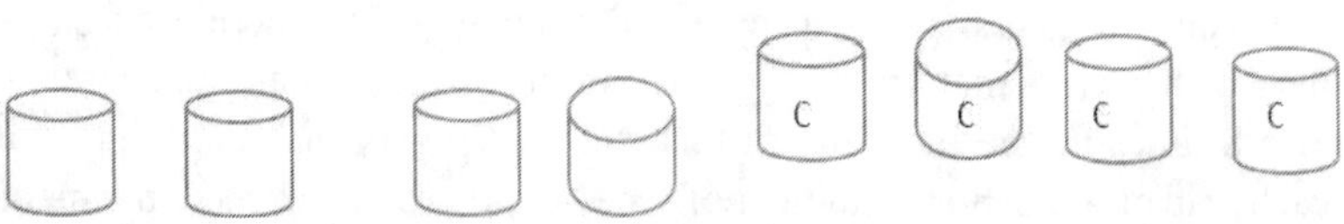

7.4.3 RAID LEVEL 2

Also known as Memory Style Error Correcting Code. (ECC).

The errors have been detected many a times by using parity bits in a memory system.

Each byte in the system has an associated parity bit with it. If the number of bits are even in a single byte then it is set to 1 (parity = 0) and if they are odd then it is set to 0 (parity = 0). If we encounter a damaged bit in any byte (i.e. if we get a 0 and it was 1 or if we get a 1 and it was 0). Then the parity of the byte changes and does not match with the stored parity. If on the other hand a stored parity bit is damaged, i.e. it is showing 1 when 0 was expected or showing 0 when 1 was expected.

Here single bit level errors are detected. Here if a single bit is damaged, then with the help of error correcting schemes, we can reconstruct the data since it has 2 or more extra bits stored for that purpose.

For Example,

First bit of each byte is stored in disk 1. Second bit in disk 2 and so on. Error correcting bits are stored in other disk. Here the disk having P in it are storing error correcting bits. If one of the disk fails, from the remaining of the byte and the error correcting bits we can restore the damaged data.

7.4.4 RAID LEVEL 3

This is also known as Bit Interleaved Parity

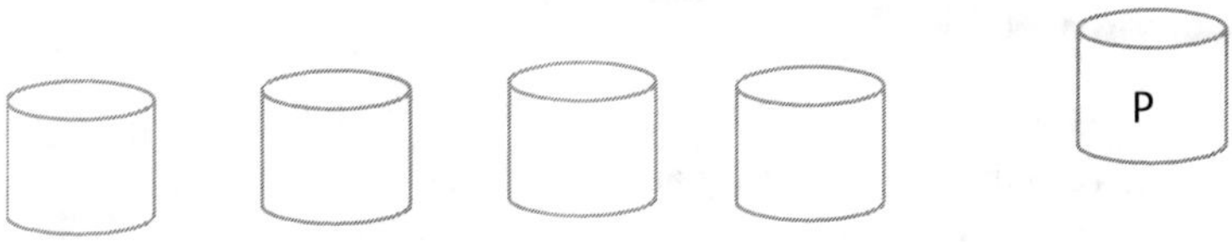

This takes care of the fact that many disk systems find out whether a sector has been damaged or not. So we use a single parity bit which can perform both error correction and error detection. We come to know the exactly which sector is damaged. Also we come to know if the sector is having bit 1 or bit 0 by computing the parity of corresponding bits from other sectors of the disk.

If the parity of the remaining bits is equal to the stored parity, then the missing bit is 0, otherwise it is 1.

Here it has the advantage over RAID 2, because instead of 3 parity disks only one is required for the same purpose. The disadvantage is that it takes more time to compute and more time for writing parity bits.

7.4.5 RAID LEVEL 4

Also known as Block Interleaved parity. This uses block level stripping as in RAID 0. It has a parity block in a separate disk for the data in the Nth other disks.

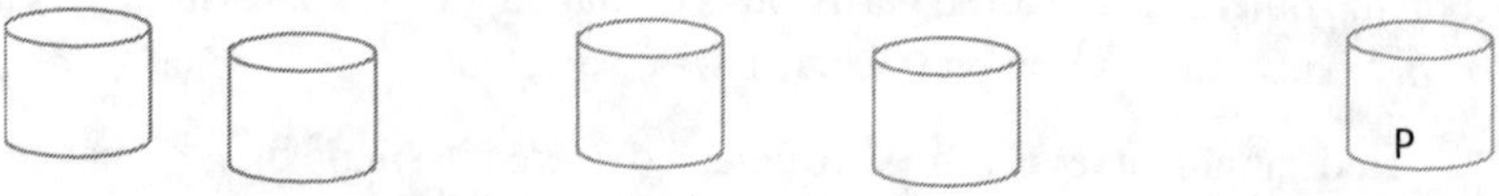

If a failure happens in any of the disks, then with the help of other blocks and the parity block we can restore back the failed disk. A block read accesses only one disk whereas other requests will be required to process other blocks. The data transfer rate might be slower but multiple read accesses can be performed parallelly to give higher overall I/O rate. Large reads can lead to higher transfer rate since disks can be read in parallel. Large writes can also lead to higher transfer rate since data and parity can be written in parallelly. Small independent writes cannot be performed in parallel.

If data is smaller than a block which has to be written then it is required that whole block is read, changes made to it and then written back. The parity block also has to be updated accordingly. This is called the read-modify-write cycle.

A single write needs 4 operations to be carried out:

2 to read the 2 old blocks (data and parity)

and 2 to write the 2 new blocks (data and parity)

7.4.6 RAID LEVEL 5

This is also known as Block Interleaved Distributed parity.

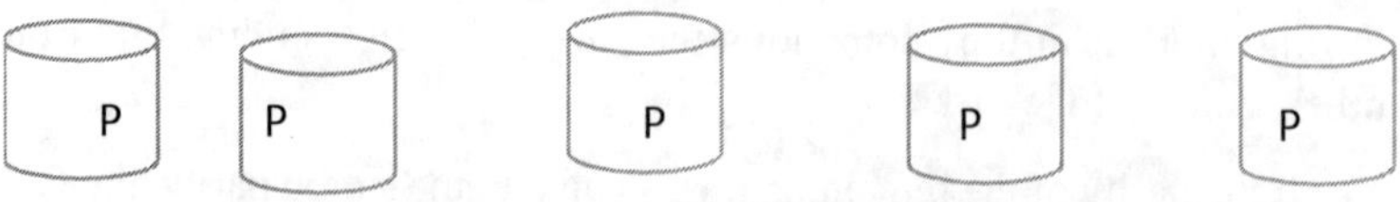

This is different from Level 4 in the sense that data and parity are spread across N + 1 disk.

In the earlier levels we saw that data is written in N disks and parity in another disk. Here for each block, one disk stores its parity and other disks store the data. Suppose we have an array of 5 disks. The parity for the Nth block is stored in disk (N mod 5) + 1. The Nth block of the other four disks store actual data for that block. A parity block cannot store the parity of the data of the same disk. Because if a disk fails then the parity is also lost and we will not be able to recreate the data.

7.4.7 RAID LEVEL 6

Also known as P+ Q redundancy Scheme.

It is much like RAID level 5, but has the capacity to recover information if multiple disks fail at the same point of time. Instead of parity, error correcting codes are stored.

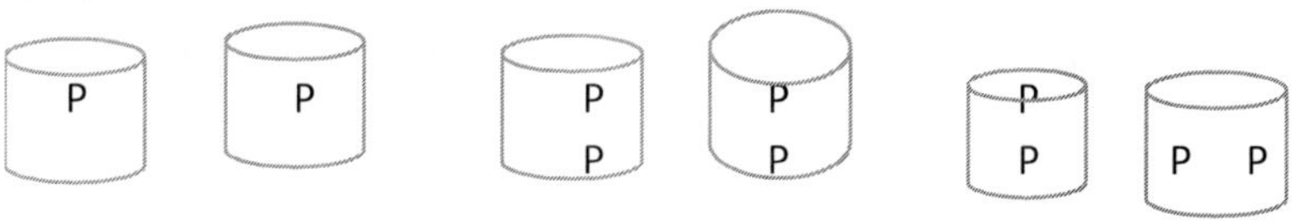

its of redundant data are stored in every 4 bits of data.

7.5 File System

Files are mapped on the physical devices by the operating system. The physical devices do not lose data if power is switched off because of their non-volatile nature. Files generally possess related information which are stored on the physical medium. The smallest allotment to a secondary storage device is a file. The data cannot be written onto a disk as it is, it has to be at least a file before it is saved.

A file may have many different type of information stored in it, such as

(1) Source program
(2) Object program
(3) Executable file
(4) Numeric data
(5) Text
(6) Video images
(7) Audio clips

A file may possess attributes, such as:

(1) Name
(2) Identifier
(3) Type

(4) Location
(5) Size
(6) Protection
(7) Time
(8) Date
(9) User modification

A file may undergo the following operations:

(1) Creating a file
(2) Writing a file
(3) Reading a file
(4) Repositioning a file
(5) Deleting a file
(6) Truncating a file
(7) Appending a file

7.5.1 File Structure

The files have to follow a required structure so that they can be understood by the operating system.

For example, if we take an executable file, then that file is supposed to be in a specified structure. So that the OS knows where to load the file, where is the address of the first instruction.

This has the disadvantage that for 5 different types of files, 5 different structures would be required.

For example, encryption may be allowed in a text file but cannot be performed on a binary file. The operating systems generally have a minimal number of file structures. For example, in UNIX everything is a file and it is a sequence of 8 bit bytes without any interpretation of bits.

Internal File structure

The Operating system would find difficulty in locating an offset within a file. So for that purpose blocks are of a particular size which is determined by the size of the sector. Any disk I/O would be carried out in units of blocks and those blocks are of uniform size. The logical records would rarely exactly match the physical record. The length of the logical record may also vary.

The solution to the above problem can be achieved by packing a number of logical records onto physical blocks. Taking an example of UNIX operating system, all files are stream of bytes. The bytes are individually addressable which can be depicted as an offset taken from beginning of the file or the offset taken from end of the file.

Here the logical record consists of 1 byte.

The OS would pack and unpack bytes into the physical disk block. If our block is of say 512 bytes then it will do as necessary. The size of the physical block, as well as the size of a logical record and the blocking technique used determine how many logical records would fit in each physical block. The disk space is allocated in terms of the physical blocks. So for the last block some space would generally be wasted.

For example, if our block is of 512 bytes, then a file size of 1739 bytes would be allocated a space of 4 blocks. Out of which 3 blocks would be occupied by 1536 bytes (3 * 512) and the 4th block will use 203 bytes (1739-1536). So 309 bytes (512-203) of the 4th block would be wasted.

7.5.2 Access Methods

(1) Sequential Access:

The simplest way in which a file can be accessed in order is one record after another.

(2) Direct Access: also known as Relative Access.

In direct access the records can be written or read rapidly without following any particular order. The file is made up of these records. The direct access method is based on the model of the disk which allows random access to any block in the file.

Here the block in a file are numbered or the records in the file are numbered. Thus, we may read block 16, then block 55, and then block 9.

(3) Indexed Access

On top of direct access method we can build an index for the file. The index can be compared to the index in the end of the book which points to various blocks. If we need to find a record in the file, then the index is searched first. From there we get the pointer to access the file and subsequently the record.

Suppose the record consists of the following:

10 bit identifier	6 bit subtype	data

The record is of = 16 bytes.

A block is made up of = 1024 bytes

The number of records that a block can have = 1024 / 16
= 64

A file is made up of 120,000 records

Size of file in bytes = 120,000 * 16
= 1,920,000 bytes

The number of blocks required to fit the file = file size/ block size
= 1920000 / 1024
= 1875 blocks

To have an index, we need to sort the file by 10 digit integer. The index can then be created which will consist of identifier in each block. The index will contain 1875 entries. These entries will be of 10 digit each.

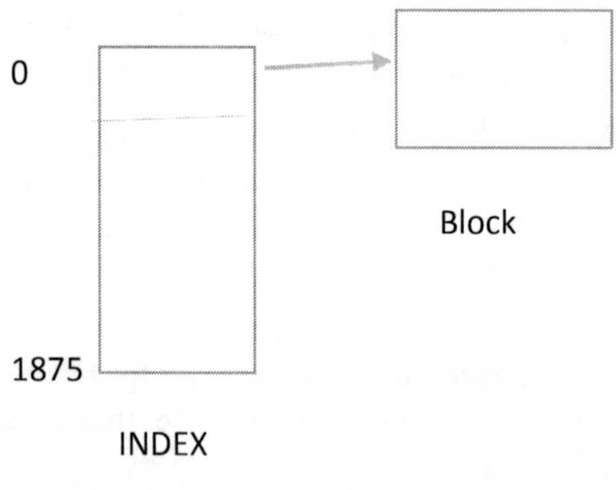

We make a search into the index, to find the subtype, and from there we get the desired block and the desired record. When an index becomes too large to handle, then we create the index of indexes.

The first level index gives a pointer to the second level index which further gives us the block.

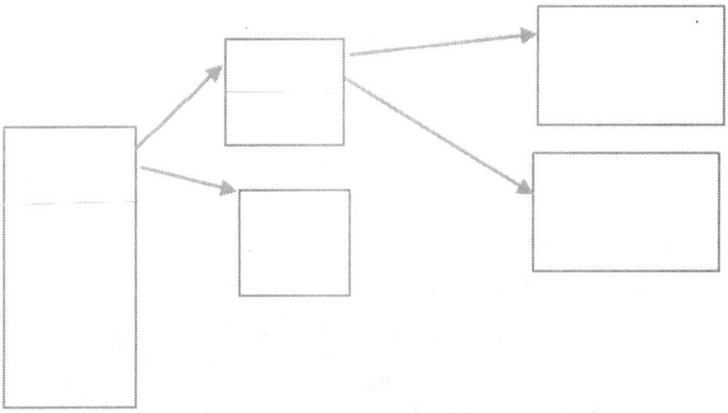

RFirst Level Index Second Level Index Blocks

7.6 Directory and Disk Structure

A disk is partitioned into quarters and each quarter can hold a file system. The partitions are also known as slices or minidisks. Any entity which has a file system in it is known as volume. The volume can consist of a subset of a device or the whole device as it is or the number of devices linked together such as in RAID.

The volume itself can be thought of as a virtual disk. Multiple operating systems may be stored on a volume and at system boot up time more than one operating system can be selected. The files which are present in a volume need to store the information about the files also. The volume may hold these entries in the table of contents or the device directory may hold such information. The device directory also holds information about files such as

Its name, location, size, type on that volume.

Storage Structure

A file system in a UNIX operating system is as follows:

At the top there is a root directory, under which we have subdirectories such as etc, dev, tmp, bin.

/(root)

/dev /bin /etc /tmp /usr

The directory holds many files and has the entries of those files. The following operation can be performed in a directory.

(1) Search a file:

The directory structure is searched to find the entry of particular file.

(2) Create a file: The directory must be able to add the information of a newly created file.

(3) Delete a file: If file is not required any more then it needs to be deleted.

(4) List a directory: The directory would need to list all the files that are present in it. And also the contents of each entry of the directory.

(5) Rename a file: If the name of a file is changed, then that needs to be updated.

(6) Traverse the file: We need to traverse the file system so that we can read any file in the directory structure.

7.6.1 Directory Structure

The directory structure may be of any one of the following:

(1) Single Level Directory
(2) Two Level Directory
(3) Tree Structure
(4) Acyclic Graph Directory
(5) General Graph Directory

(1) Single Level Directory

All files are present in the same directory.

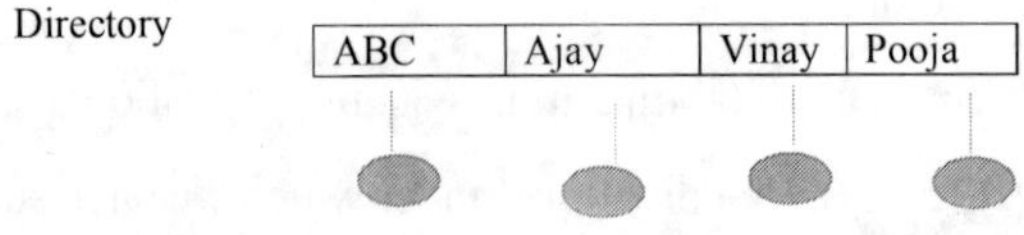

(2) Two Level Directory

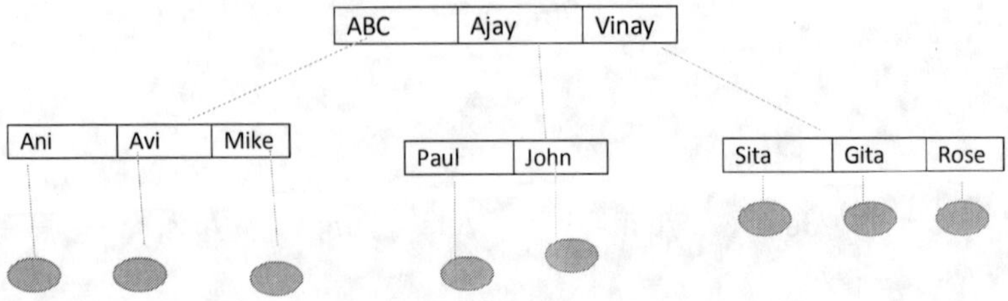

(3) Tree directory structure

If we have more than 2 levels of directories, then we need to have a tree structure.

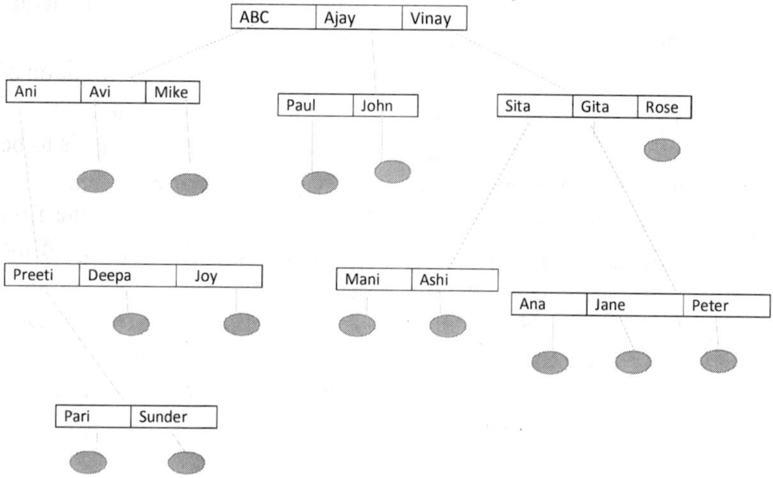

(4) Acyclic Graph Structure

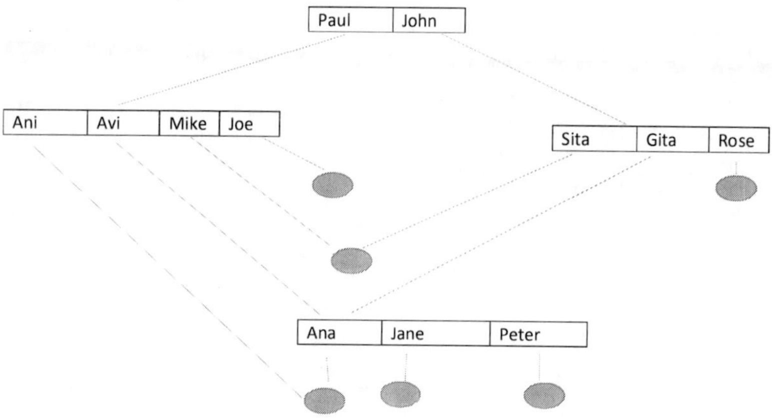

Let us assume that there are 2 persons which are working on the same project. They require that the same subdirectory should be under them or the directory which is commonly used to be shared. That shared directory or file will need to be present at 2 places at the same time.

The tree structure does not allow sharing of files. An acyclic graph has the capacity to share subdirectories and files. This graph does not contain any cycle. The same file or directory may be present in 2 different directories. In a shared file system, if one person makes changes to a file, then the other person can also see the change. If a new file is created in a subdirectory by one person then the other person can also see it.

(5) General Graph Directory

The problem with acyclic graphs is that we need to ensure that it does not have any cycles. The way to the above problem is to traverse the graph and see that there are no more references to a file.

A 0 value in the reference count would indicate that there are no more references to the file or directory. And then we will be able to delete the file. If the reference count is not 0 then it indicates that a cycle is there. On adding or deleting files, we need to ensure that a tree structure is followed. But at times it may not be able to ensure, and a graph may exist as shown below:

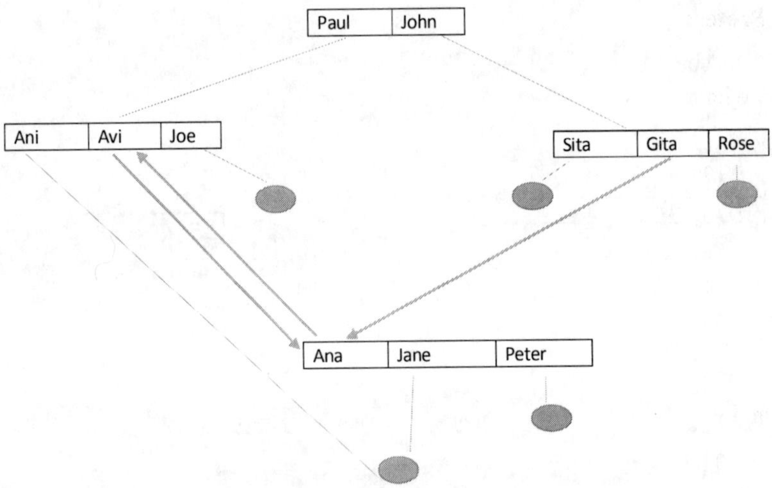

A cycle is formed between Ana and Avi.

Garbage Collection

In garbage collection, we traverse the whole file system and go on marking the components which we can access. On doing the second round we collect all the components that have not been marked and put them in a list of free spaces.

Garbage collection is used to tell us the disk spaces that can be allocated. In case there is a cycle, then the reference count will not be 0. And a file or directory may be asked for again and again. Therefore, we use garbage collection for the graph structures. An acyclic graph structure was a much better option but the disadvantage with that is that we need to ensure that a cycle does not exist whenever we add new files.

7.6.2 File Sharing

We need to take care of file sharing, naming, and protection whenever we have multiple users. We need to have special access permissions for that. So we have 3 types of users, owner, group and others in file sharing. We can also remotely share files. Earlier we had File Transfer Protocol commonly known as ftp. Now we have Distributed File System (DFS). In DFS we are able to view remote files from our local machine. WWW can access the remote files. Also the client server model is able to access files remotely by client giving requests to server.

Protection

A user who created the file would not want others to access it. Therefore, we have the following types of access:

(1) Read

(2) Write

(3) Execute

(4) Append

(5) Delete

(6) List

There is a scheme of access control which tells which file to access and with what permissions.

The file access permission in a UNIX operating system is as follows:

-rwxr-x- -x file.c

Here first alphabet is – which indicates that it is a file

Next three alphabets are rwx - which indicate the owner of the file and he has all three read, write and execute permissions.

Next three alphabets are r-x -which indicate the group of the file and people in the group have r for read permission, - for no write permission and x for execute permission.

Next three alphabets are - - x – which indicate other people, who are neither owner nor group and they have - for no read, - for no write and x for execute permission.

The owner has all the three permissions for the file file1.c. The members of the owner's group can have read and execute permissions but do not have the write permission on the file file1.c. The others do not have read or write permission, only have the execute permission for the file file1.c.

File System Implementation

There is a file control block which stores all the information related to the file including owner, permissions, location and the contents of the file.

File permissions
File dates(creation, updation)
File owner, group
File size
File Data Blocks or pointers to file data blocks

Directory Implementation

Linear List is the simplest form of implementing a directory. It has a list of files with the pointers to the block of data. In having a new file, the whole directory is searched to find out that no existing file has the same name. In case we need to delete a file, the entire directory is searched to get the space which has to be freed.

7.6.3 Allocation Methods

There are 3 allocation methods which exist for allocating the disk space to a file.

(1) Contiguous

(2) Linked

(3) Indexed

(1) Contiguous Method:

This says that each file is to have contiguous blocks (one after another) allocated on the disk The disk addresses have linear ordering on the disk.

Suppose our file is m block long and starts at a location s, then it would occupy blocks s, s+1, S+2....s+m-1. Each directory entry has information about a file and it contains the address of the starting block and the length of the allocated area.

Suppose we have,

FILE	STARTING	LENGTH
ABC	0	3
PQR	7	2
STU	10	3

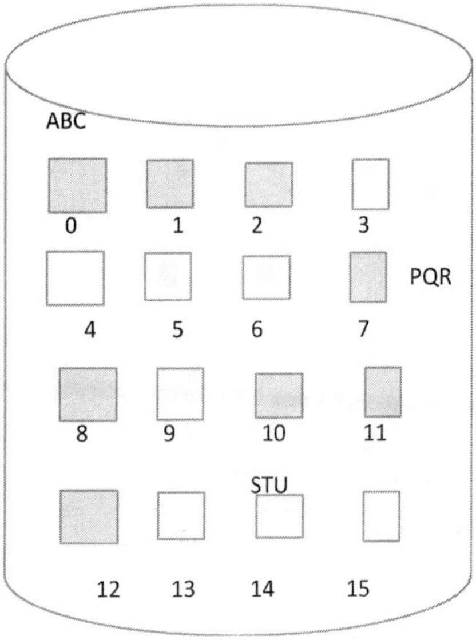

In this case we need to manage the free spaces.

In this if a new file has to be accommodated, then those many free spaces as the length of file need to be empty contiguously (one after another).

This is the case of external fragmentation and will require compaction. Also in advance we should know how many blocks does this file require.

(2) Linked Allocation

This does not require contiguous blocks. Each file has a linked list to maintain its blocks. The disk blocks of a particular file may be located anywhere, need not be one after another. The directory entry of each file contains the pointer to the first block and the last block of the file.

Suppose we have a file which is spread across the disk. Suppose its first block is 2, then it goes to block 10, then it has block 5 and finally block 12. So it is shown below how it can be implemented.

Each block contains a pointer to the next block. The user does not have any knowledge about the pointers.

DIRECTORY ENTRY

FILE	STARTING	END
ABC	2	12

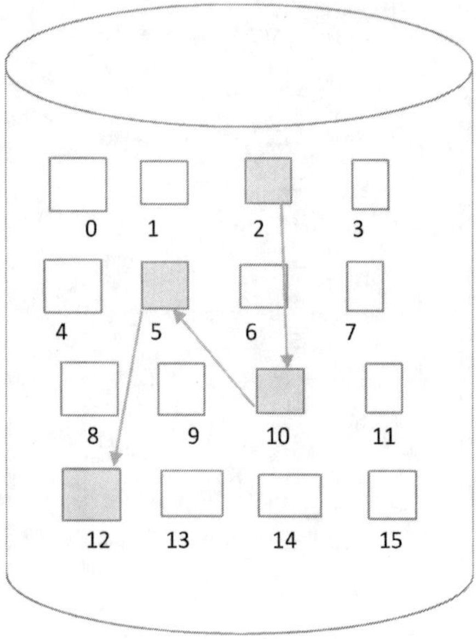

Here it does not suffer from external fragmentation. The blocks need not be free contiguously. File size also need not be available beforehand. If we create a new file, then a new entry in the directory needs to be made.

Each disk entry needs to store the pointer of the first disk block. The last pointer is given a value of null to indicate that the file is empty. When a write needs to be performed, then a free block is found and contents written on top of it and attached to the linked list of the file. To read we have to follow all the linked pointers before we reach the desired block.

(3) Indexed Allocation

This method solves the problem of sequential access as well as contiguous allocation. Here we have an Index block. This allocation guarantees that we have direct access without having external fragmentation. Any free block which is available in the disk can be granted to any file asking for more space. Indexes do not have the problem of wasting space. The pointers in an indexed allocation are more than those required in a linked allocation.

Each file has an index block associated with it. The index block of a file stores all the blocks that are used by the file in an array. The directory entry of each file containing the address of the index block of the file. Suppose a directory entry of a file has 14 as its index block. So the block 14 has an array of values of the blocks that the file is using for storing its contents. The array of blocks basically contains the pointer to that block.

When a new file is created, all its pointers are set to null. When data is written on the file, then a block is taken from the free spaces blocks and its address is stored in the index block entry. This technique supports random access without having external fragmentation. We need to decide first hand as to how big an index block should be.

DIRECTORY ENTRY

FILE	INDEX BLOCK
ABC	14

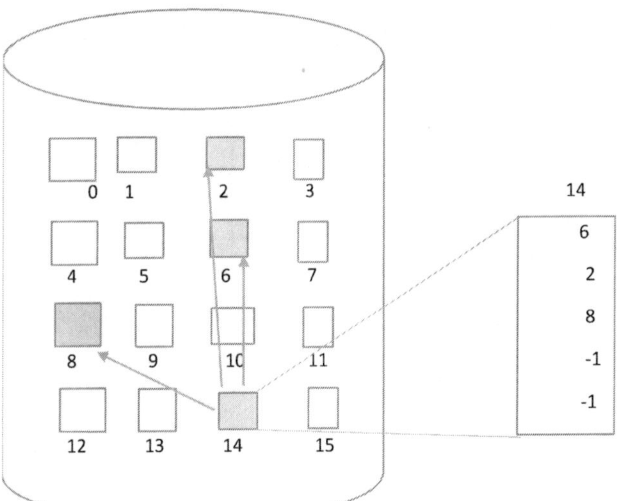

Index

Mutual Exclusion, 46, 53, 57, 59, 69, 73, 121, 127

O

P

R

S

T

U

V